WAYWARD SON

Loose and free

MARK ANTHONY

DEDICATION

To my friends Paul and Sheila Fronda, who helped me to edit this book and to my good friend Paul O'Neill who helped give it its finishing touches, I offer you my gratitude and appreciation.

To my wife Bev, I offer the love and respect that is due to a patient and loving wife. It is your indomitable spirit that has brought us this far. You have shared some difficult years through this transition and yet your hope still remains. I am deeply grateful.

Contents

Mark Anthony

Wayward Son: Loose and Free

Acknowledgements

To the staff in Baytrees Detox Unit, Yeldall Manor, Teen Challenge, Betel UK and even prison staff all across the country. For every pastor, chaplain, minister and God's other chosen servants that crossed my path and walked with me. I am in debt for your time, effort and patience. I am now walking in gratitude and may God bless you all in helping me to bring this book into completion.

Foreword

I'd been thinking about writing a book for some time, but wasn't sure what I should write about; after all, I've not done much to be proud of. I do however think that my story of redemption is something to be shared.

So, I'll start by introducing myself. I was born *'Shepard'*, but I became a *'lost sheep'*. I was born in Fareham, Hants, in 1963 with a different name; I had it shortened some time after, as I had accrued a lot of convictions and was detaching myself from my earthly father.

I have spent a lot of years in the 'wilderness', so to speak, in and out of trouble with the police, courts and prisons. I often asked myself why and so have decided to take a look at my life and I invite you to join me.

Now, it's easy to make a judgement on someone that you've just met; I've done it myself, on 'every' occasion. But, as I have learnt personally, we are only working from the information that stems from our own preconceptions; based on our own ideals, values, and beliefs. These aren't always consistent with reality, logical or even true. Normally more evidence is needed to support that which we perceive and so more, often than not, the judgement is misconstrued and inappropriate.

However, if you had thought that I had been a selfish and arrogant person, I would have taken offence; but that wouldn't have meant it wasn't true.

Our backgrounds do play a major part in our development, but the relationships we have play a bigger part. That's not to say that someone from an underprivileged family can't go on to achieve and succeed. On the contrary, with a good positive influence in our lives – anything is possible!

In my early years, I had no positive attachment. There was no one that I really looked up to as a role model; except for maybe a Sunday school teacher and my Aunt Sylvie (bless her). Instead, I struggled to cope and get what I really needed.

I make no excuse for my behaviour back then. Whether right or wrong, it has brought me to where I am today; however, at a high cost and with lots of harsh consequences and I wish to share the journey.

People sometimes let us down and things often go wrong, but we are responsible for the attitude that we have and the decisions that we make. I'm not making light of the terrible or evil actions of those that neglect, abuse and generally mistreat us. Especially, those in whom we place our trust and who are supposed to be our guardians. I'm more concerned with the effect that it has on us. We are mostly powerless over people, events and situations; but we have the ability within us to be empowered to step out of any situation.

I'm aware that I might not have been through what you have and vice versa. We all have something valuable to share. It is my wish that, no matter what you might have been through, you can identify with a need to move on and not get stuck in a place of 'darkness' without any light at the end of the proverbial tunnel.

Steps are what we take as a child and as an adult. Sometimes we fall, but the quicker that we get back up, the sooner we can get on with the journey. I have stumbled many times and sometimes I've had to be lifted back up, often at some expense or cost.

There are parts to my story that are painful and I've found it hard coming to terms with the grief, guilt, shame, anger and a whole other list of emotions. But I have and so can you dear reader!

And finally, although I do not wish to keep anything back, certain names have been omitted, as it is not my intention to cause any offence or to create any other family rifts. However, I have nothing to hide and I'm not seeking anyone's approval by refraining from the truth, so I apologize if anyone's identity is revealed because of the circumstances.

There are episodes in my life that I'd rather not remember. And yet I hope that, in sharing most of them with you, it may encourage you. I will at least have been able to put to rest that which has haunted me for a very long time.

However, I have found forgiveness in my Lord and Saviour Jesus Christ and things are being restored to me and I'm also in the process of being reconciled to the relationships that matter to me most. I love both my wife, Bev, and my children and I'm grateful for their love

I was born a sinner, but I grew a repentant heart and if this book gives you food for thought, then you might want to take a look at my 'note' at the rear of this book. God Bless!

(The author)

"A few days later this younger son packed all his belongings and moved to a distant land, and there he wasted all his money in wild living. About the time his money ran out, a great famine swept over the land, and he began to starve. He persuaded a local farmer to hire him, and the man sent him into his fields to feed the pigs. The young man became so hungry that even the pods he was feeding the pigs looked good to him. But no one gave him anything.

"When he finally came to his senses, he said to himself, 'At home even the hired servants have food enough to spare, and here I am dying of hunger! I will go home to my father and say, "Father, I have sinned...""

(Luke 15:13-18 NLT Bible)

CHAPTER ONE

Sunday school

I hated Sunday mornings, because my dad would wake me up to tidy the whole house. I'd do that and any other job that was left for me, like cutting open used cigarette ends that he'd stored up in a second-hand ashtray. He used to smoke tobacco and would keep his butts separate from the ash. I found it disgusting, but it was okay when I fancied the odd sneaky roll-up and it was my job to keep his tin full.

I remember a typical Sunday morning, as having to complete my chores and then I wasn't allowed out until all the housework was done. This involved tidying everything away in my room and the front room. I then had to dust and Hoover the three-bed roomed maisonette and do any washing up that had accumulated since the evening before.

It used to embarrass and anger me when my friends, Steve or Elliot, would come round for me and my dad would send them away until I'd finished. I would usually find one of my mates over in one of the neighbouring fields, adjacent to the flats that I lived in.

There was a church nearby and we used to play around their building, climbing onto the corrugated tin roof and then jumping over the surrounding fence, onto the grass. On one occasion, one of the leaders came out and I was invited in to the Sunday youth service. I looked at my mate and laughed, trying to 'save face'. I was embarrassed because I use to 'take the Mick' out of those going to church and I was thinking that I wasn't going to let a Bible-basher start preaching to me about how much God loves me and how I should confess my sins.

Repentance was a word that I didn't understand and I certainly wasn't aware of any sins that I may have been committing. However, the rumour was that they used to dish out goodies and have day trips in the summer and I didn't get to go on holiday much. I thought that maybe I should give it a go and see what was in it for me.

So, here I was, walking into the small church hall for the first time and it was quite daunting, as I didn't know quite what to expect. I felt nervous, especially around people that I didn't know. Yet, it had an atmosphere that made me want to stay.

I don't recall any names (no excuse for my ignorance), but it was a long time ago and I think all the drink and drugs that I've used over a long period of time can affect the short and long term memory. But, I do recall how I felt amongst those good people earlier on in my life and how I longed to feel that way for a long time after.

I was introduced to a big book, with some memorable characters from a lifetime ago, long before mine. They were to make an awesome impression on me. They were a real mixture of men and women, but they all seemed to have a typical thread that ran through them. In ancient times when all the odds seemed against them, courage and honour was what prevailed in their lives. That book was the Bible.

I didn't see myself in any way as a particularly brave person, but I did long to be remembered as a man of honour and strength.

There was a story of a man who lived in a village that was surrounded by those who wanted to take his life because the people looked up to him. He did no wrong as such; although he took pride in doing what he thought was right and had a weakness for beautiful women. This led to the man's demise, but not before bringing down the house on his enemies. His name was Samson.

In another chapter, a man, the smallest of his brothers and not known as a fighter, took out a giant, who was also an enemy of his people. He saved his people from being overthrown in a war that was going against them. This man had been a humble shepherd, soon became a warrior and then turned into a king. His name was David.

One of my favourites though was the story of a man who, when born, was supposed to have been put to death because it was told that a man would come to rescue his people from a place of slavery. (The ruler at the time thought that he could stop this, but didn't have the power to come against God and his power.) His name was Moses.

I read that this God was a loving God and had a plan to rescue his people, with his strong arm, from their place of slavery.

I listened to the stories and imagined myself as that kind of hero, who was sent to save the people from that which was a threat and would oppose them. Learning about the Bible left an impression on me, of how God cares for his people. It's a record of his provision and protection, as he led a chosen nation out of oppression.

Yeah, this was probably the best time of the week for me and I looked forward to going each week, to get away from the coldness at home. I can't say there weren't any good times at home because there were, but more often than not, bad stuff happened, rather than good.

I was given an illustrated pamphlet that showed the path of a man's life, which leads to his own destruction. It detailed how, whilst growing up, this man is walking down a road that is signposted with all the things that might distract him from his journey. He tries to stay on the right path, but makes some wrong choices that inevitably lead him to the wrong destination. It was frightening because he ended up in a place called 'Hell'. I believe this was meant as a warning and a deterrent to me, but I never listened and didn't like to be told what to do.

My dad was always doing that, shouting at me, aggressively and threateningly. I hated it!

Yet, there in that little room, far away from any of his or anyone else's abuse, I was safe and the people seemed to care about me. It was the one place in my life that I felt loved, accepted and secure and I longed to find that security at home and in my own family.

Now before I go any further with my story, I want to ask you a question – do you believe in good and evil? If there is a God, then would he allow the wicked things to happen the way that they do? More importantly, why doesn't he stop them from happening? I believe that man (or woman) made a choice and has been suffering the consequences since!

CHAPTER TWO

Abandoned

I grew up in a neighbourhood which had a hierarchy from the top-end of the street to the bottom. It didn't make a difference to us who lived down at the other end. At one end was the nice row of houses and gardens with freshly cut grass and at the other was a block of maisonettes - an ugly tenement building that ruined the local landscape.

This is where I lived and it didn't matter though, because it wasn't about having a nice house or a mum or dad who was there. Everyone there had something in common and it was the dysfunction in our relationships, which we could all relate to. It was poor living but we got on with it, the best way that we could.

The flats were encompassed by a surrounding copse and fields where the families' kids would play. A bit further on was the park with a woodland area attached to it. That was where we played when we wanted to get away from the realities of our own home lives.

Most, if not all, families had a spouse that was missing; either absent or caught up in the throes of abandonment or separation. My family was no different and the marriage of my mother and father was on melt-down. Constant streams of abuse flowed, rather than the love and nurture needed to make any relationship grow in a family.

My father worked in the stores, in one of the navy's depots for the Royal Navy Reserve. Christmas time seemed great because we got to sample the good fare, such as tenderloin steak and giant hot dogs, which was a treat after the usual stuff that my mum would knock up. I didn't know at the time that she struggled with the housekeeping because it had been mentioned that my tight father spent most, if not all, his wage on other things, such as porn and trips to seedy spots in London with his mates.

From a very young age, I would take care of my two little sisters: Kate, and Mandy, my baby sister. My mum would still be in bed when I got up to go to school, so I felt it was my job to look after my sisters. Mandy would wake up with a dirty nappy and so I got on and changed it. Then I'd take care of dressing them and give them breakfast, before going to school. I was seven years old and attending the junior school that was opposite where we lived.

On one occasion, I decided that I'd play 'bartender', behind the cocktail bar that decorated our lounge. I say 'lounge', but we lived in a three-bed roomed flat, which had a kitchen, bathroom (with toilet) and sitting room – nothing as lavish as a lounge.

It was more like something out of 'Only Fools and Horses' on TV. I proceeded to pour drinks out for my little sisters, who seemed to be enjoying the game that I had put on for them.

Sometime after, I was in school during a games session when I heard the shouts of my angry father. I was terrified, as he was a big overbearing man at the best of times. He found me at the top of a climbing frame in the assembly hall. He screamed at me to come down and I could see the looks of concern on the teachers' faces, who were trying to placate him. My initial reaction was to stay at the top of the apparatus, out of reach of his fury; but I knew this would just anger him more, so I came down in the hope that he wouldn't kill me; at least not in front of my teachers.

"What the hell do you think you're doing, getting your sisters drunk? Mandy has gone to hospital and if anything happens to her, then God help you!" he said, dragging me out of the school to his car and driving us to the Royal Naval Hospital.

My mum was there, crying, as my little sister lay motionless in the hospital bed. She had managed to get hold of some bleach from the upstairs bathroom and had consumed some on top of the alcohol that I had given her. Fortunately, she had a stomach pump and no serious damage was done. I thank God that she survived, but it left me with some serious guilt feelings over how my lack of responsibility had nearly killed my baby sister.

Life continued to be chaotic and I was often finding myself in some kind of trouble. Like the time I accidentally shut the fingers of one of my old school girlfriends in a door. Her father was phoned and asked to come and collect her. I was outside the headmistress's office door because I had to give an explanation as to how I'd managed to catch the girl's fingers in the door. It felt bad enough, but when I saw a policeman come round the corner, I nearly lost control of myself. It was accepted as an accident and I was let off, much to the disapproval of the poor girl. He was the local bobby, called Dick, and it wouldn't be the last time that he and I would have any dealings.

My father went off to sea with the RNR (Royal Navy Reserve) and things didn't seem so bad. Mum seemed happier when dad wasn't around. At least we didn't have to experience his mood swings that were also violent.

I witnessed the kind of emotional abuse that my mother was put through and it wasn't nice to see the pain that she went through. But, I wasn't in a position to protect her, as I was neither aware of what was going on or able to do anything about it.

I remember that we were driving along one day, with my mum in the front of the car and my dad with us in the back. He was having a go at her, when suddenly he threatened to drop me and my sisters off on the corner and drive the car through a wall, with them both in it. This was typical of his aggressive behaviour and seemed much the norm.

I guess that I inherited that same behaviour and was constantly getting into fights at school and at home, with kids from neighbouring territories. Although, in fairness, at school there was a gang of boys that terrorized the other pupils and a group of us would oppose their bullying. This would have an adverse effect on me in times to come.

I found it tough being a kid, trying to survive in a world where everything and everyone seems to be against you. I felt no love from my parents and I was alone in a world that seemed to want to hurt me. I had to be strong and was determined not to show weakness; but I had the wrong idea of what courage really was.

It was about this time that I had my first taste of offending behaviour. If I'd known where it was going to lead, I might have changed my attitude to breaking the law. Stealing came to me so easily and, although I knew it to be wrong, I was drawn to it naturally, with no coercion from any peers.

There were some shops nearby to where we lived and I remember wanting some sweets, so I went into the Co-op and stole a small chocolate bar. I was afraid that I might get caught, but got caught up in the thrill of getting away with it. So I did it again on a number of occasions, but one day the store manager saw me and took me to one side. I was very apologetic and swore that I wouldn't do it again if he didn't tell my parents (especially my dad). I was let off with a warning, something that I chose to ignore. My parents weren't very giving and, if I wanted something, I would just take it.

1970 was probably the most crap year of my life and it all fell apart for me from there. Everything must have been too much for my mum, what with being in an unloving relationship and having three children to bring up without my father's support.

I was seven years old when I came home from school one day and found that I couldn't get in. My sister and I waited on the doorstep, until my father could be reached and came home. He opened the door to a quiet and cold house and we all walked in. My dad walked into the kitchen as we raced upstairs to get out of our school uniforms. When I came downstairs my dad was in the kitchen, sitting at the table with his back to me. I walked to the table and saw what appeared to be a letter crumpled up on it. My father was saying something through muffled words. I looked at his face and he was crying.

"She's gone," he said. "She's left us," was all he kept saying.

At first, it didn't register in my young mind that he was talking about my mum. I didn't want to believe or even conceive that my mum would leave me behind.

My father was overcome by the misery of my mother's departure and became unbearable to live with. For the first couple of months, it was uncertain whether she would return home. I really missed my mum and didn't like being without her. My dad would drive us around to all her friends and those who had known her, to look for her, but it became obvious that she had long gone.

This affected my outlook and my school work, as my home life had been shattered. I became very angry and was unable to manage my feelings. I hated school and was always being drawn into fights with particularly nasty pupils.

One gang that I had problems with was led by a boy called 'Savage' and he used to make my life hell. He must have been a miserable kid because I don't ever remember a smile on his face, unless he has trying to put fear in me. I upset the gang one time and they laid in wait for me outside the school gates. I couldn't avoid them because my house was literally yards away from the school. I walked up to them, trying to muster any courage that I could find, but really I was trying very hard not to shake with the fear that I felt inside. I was outnumbered and got beaten up, much to the disapproval of my father, who had been a spectator. He called me in and suggested that I go back and fight or that he would give me a hiding.

One of my mum's sisters lived nearby and I enjoyed visiting and spending time with my Aunt Sylvie. She was like a surrogate mum and my uncle Mike was a top bloke. I would have loved to have lived with her and she even tried to adopt me when my mother left, but my old man wasn't having any of it. That's not to say it would have been easy, because my Aunt Sylvie isn't the type that you'd mess about with and would soon give me a clout around the head if I messed about.

However, Kate and I were less fortunate and my father decided that one of his sisters would be our guardian while my dad went to work. My father's older sister, Phyllis, got the job of taking care of us for a while. She was an unmarried mother with one child and lived at home with my Nan, who was getting on in years. I didn't get to know a grandfather, as both my parents' fathers had died.

Aunt Phil was a tall, domineering woman, whose face was hawk-like and she was scary. She'd bully my sister into eating meals as Kate wasn't eating properly because she wasn't coping without our mum. And she had a son, a year older than me, who would take out his frustration on me. My Nan was a scary character too; she was a medium, who claimed that she was in contact with the dead and this caused an intense and eerie feeling about the house.

My cousin, Brett, was a nasty b-----d and was always being spiteful to Kate and myself; he bullied me and I really wanted to kick his ass (if I could have got away with it), but I decided instead that we had to get away from there.

One evening, while we were sitting at the dinner table and everyone had finished eating; Kate wanted to be excused from finishing her meal. Aunt Phil tried to force Katy to eat the dinner that she clearly had had enough of and she was sick on her plate. My aunt pushed my sister's face into it and I was appalled. I really wanted to do something hurtful back. Later that evening, when my father came to pick us up, my aunt gave him her version. My dad hit my sister for misbehaving and I felt helpless as I looked on, angry but afraid. We hated it there for all kinds of reasons and I kept on at my dad to not let us stay there.

A year later, my dad decided to pack a bag and move to London - without us. Kate and I were shipped across Portsmouth Harbour to another of my dad's sisters. My aunt and uncle managed a pub in Land port. They had a larger family, comprising of three older sons, a daughter and the youngest boy, who was almost a year younger than me. At first, I thought it would be great, living above a pub. It seemed so exciting to be part of another family and one that seemed to be doing so well.

Kate and I were enrolled at a local school that was named after the great author whose birthplace was in the city, Charles Dickens. My youngest cousin was in the same year as me, but we didn't get on too well at first. He was the youngest and had been spoilt. The fighting between us continued at school and at home. It was strange because indoors we were fine, apart from the usual sibling rivalry, but outside we clashed. It might have been because the local young girls had been giving him all their attention, until I turned up. I was a fresh-faced sensitive kid, who appeared different. I might have looked good on the outside, but on the inside I was in turmoil. Besides, I felt that neither Kate nor I were really welcome and that we were there more out of duty to my father.

This was where I had my first taste of drinking. In between their shifts, they would go upstairs to rest, but my cousins and I would play downstairs in the bars and cellar. All that drink was enticing and I would steal the odd bottle of Pils lager and a cigar.

On the way to school, I would creep out of the off-sales, after nicking a Castella cigar out of one of the cigar tins and a box of matches. There was a park on the way to school and that is where I'd take time out to sample my 'steals'. As I was laying back on a slide, trying to inhale the smoke, an elderly woman came up and reprimanded me. The silly old sort threatened to tell my parents and I gave her backchat with: "You'll have a long way to go." But I still hoped that my aunt and uncle would not find out that I was stealing, never mind drinking and smoking at the grand age of eight.

Kate and I dealt with our emotions in different ways; she internalised hers and became withdrawn and I expressed mine in anger and offending behaviour. The truth is, I was lonely, hurting and afraid!

I had developed a hunger deep in my soul to be loved, accepted and approved of. I didn't know it at the time, but I craved the love and attention of anyone who might be willing to give it to me. There were a lot of girls living nearby who caught my eye and I wasn't short of girlfriends. But I could never stay in any relationship too long without something going wrong and it ending. It was all quite innocent though and kissing was about all that I had ever experienced.

At such a young and vulnerable age, I was exposed to different forms of abuse. On one occasion, one of the guys who drank in my aunt's pub, asked to take me out for the day. He had a house in Southsea, a particularly wealthy area where hotels were situated. We had a day on the seafront, with him paying for ice creams and trampolines on the beach, before taking me back to his house. On this occasion, nothing untoward happened and he gained my trust. He then arranged to take me out again, but this time it was to a nearby house. It felt really intense and he tried to get me into a bedroom, but I became scared and said: "I want to go home."

Fortunately, he took me back and I never saw him again, at least not alone. It was a frightening experience, but I couldn't share it because he hadn't assaulted me and I wasn't sure that I'd be believed.

I was interested in girls, but apart from playing a childish game of 'you show me yours and I'll show you mine', I'd never gone beyond that line. (Although, I would always cheat and refuse to play my part in it, as soon as I'd seen what I wanted.) I hadn't yet experienced any further involvement with the opposite sex and was more interested in exploring bombsites or derelict buildings.

As a young boy, being exposed to the nakedness of the female form was a wakeup call to my sexuality and I was eager to see more. I'd seen the porn magazines, which my father used to stash away in his wardrobe although, in my innocence, I wasn't ready for it. But, I was keen to please and be approved of, especially by my father, who had introduced me to the female form.

"Have you seen one of these before?" he asked, shoving a pornographic picture into my face, of someone familiar to me – minus her underwear and exposing her genitalia.

"Of course I have," I said, not wanting to look inferior to him.

The truth was I had seen a girl naked before. I was eight when I first experimented with sex and she was fifteen, although I wasn't able to complete the act of intercourse, as I was still very immature. The only problem was that she was my cousin and so it was sordid and left me with deep feelings of guilt. Why she chose to reveal her nakedness to me (and more) is a question I was never able to ask or even have answered because of the shame that I felt.

Kate and I lived in Pompey for a couple of years, before coming back home to Gosport. All this had happened by the age of ten and I wasn't aware that I wasn't even responsible for most of it. I just thought I must be bad for things like this to happen to me. And so I carried this belief around with me. I truly believed that I actually deserved to be punished and that I was to blame for my mum leaving and my father being unemployed. After all, he had to give up his job in London, where he'd been happy. He was a shadow of the man that I'd known and became increasingly lonelier.

I understand that it must have been hard for my mum, being with a man who would not give her the love or support that she needed. It was even harder for me, because I couldn't just get up and go!

Rejection is tough, whether it's real or imagined. I wasn't going to let anyone get close to me anymore because I believed that I would get hurt or abused and no one would get close enough to me again to show me any different.

CHAPTER THREE

Copse Lane

At some time in 1974, we moved back into the flat that my dad had kept whilst we had all been away and I was put back into the school right on our doorstep.

This made me feel anxious as to what lay ahead. It felt strange being back in that house without my mum. My dad had tried to replace her with different women, but they never stayed. I believed that I had had a part in that because I would say things like:

"You're not my mum," and "My dad still loves my mum."

My father had to give up work to look after us properly and I guess, somewhere in all that, I appreciated it. So much so, that I refused to go and live with my mum who had suddenly turned up on the scene. I won't deny that she had remembered me at a previous Christmas time and had bought me a chopper bike that was my pride and joy

I was playing outside my Nan's one day when a well dressed lady, who looked familiar, walked past. I suddenly became aware of who it was and rushed to my Nan's front door.

"I want to see my mum," I pleaded with my Nan.

"So do I!" she retorted, trying to hide the fact that my mum was there, as I pushed past her and ran into the front room.

My mum was sitting on my Nan's couch and I found it hard to believe she was even there. She burst into tears as I ran into her arms and she said that she had come back for us.

Every fortnight she would come down and collect Kate and me. We would go back to her home in Bristol. She managed a sweet shop and had met another man called Dave. He was an engineer and an intelligent man who had become a dad to my baby sister, Mandy. I did look forward to being spoilt by them both, but I thought my mum was trying to buy my love.

I was angry with my mum for leaving me and when she mentioned that she would have us both living with her again...I told my dad. My dad's temper was very short, but it got worse when my mum turned up one day and took my sister, Kate, and left me with my dad.

All his anger was now directed at me and I felt so alone in that cold house with no love. I didn't mean to do wrong and was constantly trying to avoid his dark moods; but often found myself cowering in fear as he would dish out his violent assaults on my young body.

He was angry but he let my sister Kate go with my mum. As for me, I believed that he had looked after us and stayed with my dad. I was worried because I felt that he would be made homeless if I left him alone in a three bedroom house meant for a family. So my sister went off to enjoy her life with mum and the sweetshop and I stayed behind with dad and his anger.

If that wasn't bad enough, I had trouble at school with the same bullies. It had all started because I had stood up for my sister and another weaker guy, who had been singled out with a disability. Yet I was always the one outside the headmaster's office getting told off, with a gang waiting outside the school gate to give me a 'hiding'. My dad's response to this was to come out of the house and make me fight the one that had just beaten me up, again. I couldn't win because, if I refused, he'd beat me. He was twisted because one minute he'd say:

"I can beat you, but no one else can."

I did find this comforting, in a perverse way, because I thought my dad cared for me deep down.

It was around this time that I first tried my hand at writing some poetry, which was titled 'A Loving Father.' My dad didn't seem too impressed though, as it depicted a father with unconditional love and I think my dad thought that I was just getting back at him. His response was:

"Quite a little poet, aren't you!" he said as he threw the screwed up sheet of paper back at me.

This made me believe that my sensitivity was a weakness and I hesitated to express any feelings like that again, to him or another. Yet once again I was left with some strong emotions that I didn't know how to manage.

I loved to get out of the house and explore surrounding territories with a pal and there were a number of woods nearby that we would venture into.

One time, a mate and I were trekking through a copse on our bikes, when a guy dressed in black leathers approached us. At first there was no need for alarm, as he seemed friendly enough. But my suspicion was aroused when he pointed out a safety pin that was holding the broken fly on my trousers together. I was instantly alarmed and said to my friend,

"Quick, get out of here; he's a sex-case!"

We rode off as quickly as our bikes would take us. He followed us and it was like a nightmare because, even though he was walking behind the bikes and we were sprinting on, he seemed to be gaining on us. Terrified, I banged on my front door and shouted for my dad. He looked out of the upstairs bathroom window and shouted

"Where's your f-----g key?"

I managed to tell him that I was being followed and he could see that I was panicking as I stammered out the words. My dad came running down the stairs, out the front door and ran off, chasing the pervert that had been bothering us. I was pleased to see my dad catch up with the monster and grab him. But this was short lived because, after the police were called, he was let off without a warning. I feared that he would do it again and someone else wouldn't be so fortunate. I wasn't to know that this wasn't the last that I had seen of him or of the adverse effect that it had on me.

In the flats that I lived in, there were sixteen families that lived in close quarters and we mostly we all got on, unless I did something reckless or rude, like the time I squirted one of the neighbours. I remember a lady called Sis, who had a young daughter called Alison. The mother was standing on her front doorstep one morning and she used to give me an earful about my behaviour.

On one occasion, I was on my way to the shops, running an errand for my father. I was holding in my hand a recently filled up water pistol and, as she went to say something, I gave her a full barrel in the face. She wasn't impressed and Ali and I didn't get to talk much after that, until many years later, when she became my first real girlfriend.

My mum still arranged for me to stay with her during the summer holidays and one of my favourite memories was the time spent in Bangor on Dee. Her new husband, Dave, was an engineer and they had been allocated a bungalow to live in, alongside the river Dee, which he was building a bridge over. We used to play and camp out alongside the river and it was like something out of 'The Famous Five', sitting around a fire, telling ghost stories and trying to scare the crap out of each other. My bravery would be tested when it was time to take a 'pee'.

Mum and I used to go to bingo in a local church hall and she would share her fags. This was probably one of the closest times to my mum, and even Dave tried to care for me. He bought me clothes and taught me some engineering, in the workshop that he had at home. He had a lathe and a set of other tools, which he used to make miniature versions of construction tools, the kind that you'd find on a site. He'd also built his own brick furnace or kiln in the garden, to do the moulding. I wasn't particularly keen on Dave, although he seemed a nice man, he seemed a bit of a 'stiff' to me. My sisters had taken to him though and my mum found security in him for a while, so I went back to Gosport and my father's house.

I noticed that my friends had mothers and fathers who had stayed together and they came across as loving, supportive, and even fun. This made me wonder why it wasn't like this at home for me.

All this had happened during my junior years and I was starting to believe that something was wrong with me. This was all too much to take on and fear had crept in, alongside disbelief and doubt. My self-esteem plummeted, as did any faith that things would get any better.

My attitude was formed in those formative years. I had a deep sense of abandonment, coupled with an intense fear of separation, which would prevent me from committing to any future relationships. I resented any authority and I didn't really trust anyone. I was afraid of being rejected.

CHAPTER FOUR

Somebody Stop This

In 1975, I moved up to the 'big' school and was accepted at Brune Park Comprehensive. Things didn't change as I moved up to the seniors. I was a sensitive boy and was well aware that I wasn't developing physically as fast as some of the others.

I didn't excel in any particular sport either and wasn't involved with any team activities. I just didn't have the kit and I thought Nike was just the name of some American president. I certainly wasn't privileged with wearing the kit of my favourite team - Pompey. Instead, I had to search through some box that was full of shorts and vests that didn't fit and made me stand out like some sort of 'doughnut'.

It didn't help that, because of my father's low income, he dressed me in not so particularly fine clothes. I use to have to wear Rupert the Bear trousers and tanned winkle pickers that my dad had a certain appeal for, but I loathed them. It was embarrassing, going back to school after the summer holidays and everyone was kitted out in the latest fashion, but I felt on display with clothes that looked fresh in the fifties.

I always had a girlfriend though and would get the attention of the pretty girls in my class, as if they wanted to mother me in some way. But I found this embarrassing and didn't like to get too close – for fear of getting hurt!

It had been mentioned to my father that I was an intelligent boy that just didn't apply himself. Instead, because of my behaviour in class, I found myself on regular 'report' and had to get it signed by the tutor in every lesson. I then had to take it home and show my father how well I'd behaved. The thing is, I had anger issues and wouldn't be told what to do… by anyone.

I rebelled against all authority and just wouldn't listen to anybody. Some days I would be well behaved and would get positive and encouraging comments like 'excellent' or 'very good'. These were allowed to be run past my Father. On the other hand, the bad ones never made it for my dad's scrutiny. Instead I forged his signature and then returned it to my house head.

I found it tough in the senior school and constantly felt like I couldn't fit in. I lacked confidence because of a low self-esteem that I'd developed. I was often immobilized with frustration and anger. The truth is I was afraid and most of my fear was because of my father and his behaviour.

On the way to school each morning, I had to watch my back because I used to get jumped by kids going to other schools, that were trying to make a name for themselves and also because I had to cross the path of others that were going to neighbouring schools. This was how I came to meet a couple of brothers who, like me, lived with their dad.

Paul was the elder of the two, but his brother, Chris, was the nastier of the two. We'd have fights and most times they'd win, but on some occasions, I would come out of it the winner.

We did become friends though, when they moved into the same block as me, and Chris and I would do a lot of things together.

I got my first conviction in 1978, for shoplifting and was given a caution, but I had other things on my mind. Such as, my old man who had been accused of exposing himself to young girls from one of our bedroom windows and I had to live in that same house. I'd actually found some hidden photos of girls in explicit poses, whilst rummaging through a wardrobe one time. I was constantly abused and picked on because of what he had been accused of and I just wanted to run away.

I watched helplessly as an angry father took out his rage on my dad, for being accused of exposing himself to the guy's daughter. The feelings of disgust, shame and betrayal were enough, but I also had to deal with the bullies who had tarred me with the same brush and would taunt me with:

"You're 'Dirty Dick's' son!"

All this and then he had to go and take it one step further.... Things really started to go tits up, just after my fifteenth birthday.

I walked into my father's bedroom one morning with a pot of tea that I always made him before going to school. Lying next to him was a girl, with her clothes off and looking at me with a smile on her face. She was only a few years older than me and I found it embarrassing, especially when my father said,

"Meet your new mum."

I've got to say that I wasn't impressed and retorted, "You got to be kidding....this tart?"

He jumped naked out of the bed and went to hit me, but I ducked and left the room. This was nuts because it wasn't the first time that my dad had a relationship with a girl much younger than him.

There had been another girl called Jackie, who I had liked and got on with, but I think she may have come to her senses. I'm not saying it's wrong to have a relationship with someone younger than yourself and of 'age', but it's very unrealistic because when you're a kid you should do as kids do and when you're a man, ditto!

My father's new wife, Nikki, was a classic example of the wicked stepmother and I loathed her. Unlike her, I wasn't jealous about my father's love, because I wasn't feeling any. He beat me up, as if I was a man, punching me to the floor and telling me to get up and fight. He even suggested that I wasn't a man until I could take him into the garden and go a few rounds with him.

She seemed threatened by me though and was constantly getting me into trouble, by accusing me of things that I hadn't done. She also seemed to be envious of the freedom that I may have seemed to have had as a teenager. I believe that she was looking for some security from my father and, because of the age difference, she found she was lacking in other important areas of her life. She was only a teenager herself and, being only three years older than me, it must have been hard for her watching me go out with mates and having fun.

All this aside, I thought she was a complete bitch and this didn't change when my little brothers and sisters came. Although, I have to give my dad credit there, whatever he may have been in the past, he took to fatherhood better second time around and seemed to leave the nasty stuff behind him. I was happy for my little brothers as I didn't want them to go through what I had and felt protective over them. I just got on with it and stayed away from home as much as possible, letting them get on with the new family life.

I would go anywhere to get away from the house; it just didn't feel like a home. I even used to revisit my Aunty Phil, who was now an alcoholic and liked to interfere in her son's relationships. He would retaliate by trying to strangle her. (What a dysfunctional family I had.) Brett had become a target to local bullies too because his mum was overbearing and would accompany him everywhere. I felt sorry for him and would plead with the 'Forton' boys to leave him alone because I was on friendlier terms with them. He started to smack his old mum around and I lost respect for him and decided to leave him to his own fate.

CHAPTER FIVE

Numbing the Pain

At fifteen, I started to skive off school and would go to a wood nearby with a small group of others. It was here that I first started using solvents to change how I felt. At last I had found an escape and I believed that this was the answer to all my problems, as I didn't have to face them.

I also started to get into music and was listening to the Clash, Stranglers and the Sex Pistols. The message of anarchy echoed in my behaviour and it was a revelation of things to come. I truanted, from half way through my fourth year and all the way through my fifth, and so wasn't able to sit my O levels.

I'd met a lad called Simon, who was dressed in red bondage trousers (straps held both trouser legs together), black leather and Doc Martins. I use to go round to his home, a tidy little semi-detached house, off Copse Lane. His mum and dad seemed quite posh, but Simon used to rebel against them, in the way he dressed, acted and thought. Sometimes, when they went off to work, I'd go round to his house and get him up. He always had a glue bag under his bed and would put one of his albums on full-volume and our day would begin. One time, there were a couple of us truanting from school and we'd gone back to his for something to eat. One of his pals, a lad named Shaun, decided to crap in the cat tray. You should have seen the look on Simon's mum's face when she came home. She walked in the back door, looked down at the tray and shouted "Duchess!" We all rolled up, as the 'turd' was bigger than the cat.

I'd turn up at school for the register, then slip out a side gate and go and steal a pot of Evostik glue from a local garage or superstore. I'd then spend the day getting off my nut on a bag of glue. This would cause me to hallucinate and some of them were scary, I'd even have conversations with people who weren't there.

I started using solvents because I wanted to be approved of by those that I felt might accept me and I thought that it gave me confidence. I seemed to lose all my fears up the woods, with the glue bag in my hand and enjoyed pushing it to the next level. In the back of my mind, I knew that it might be dangerous and this gave it an edge. I heard things like 'one day you're going be a strong man' and had premonitions of things to come and people that I'd meet. I also nearly lost my life because of asphyxiation, but something brought me back to life and reality.

This wasn't my first taste of demonic influence though, as my dad had participated in an Ouija board once and that had scared the crap out of me too.

On one occasion I'd been playing in my room when I heard a scream downstairs from Evelyn, my dad's girlfriend at the time. I asked what the matter was and she mentioned that a chair had been pulled out from beneath her whilst she was using it to stand on, to close a window. I thought 'yeah right', as no one was there. Later that day, she'd been upstairs in the bathroom, rinsing some washing in the bath, and then she came downstairs and started acting hysterical. When I asked her what was wrong, she mentioned that she'd just seen Tess in the bathroom mirror. Tess had been my dad's girlfriend previously and there had been talks about marriage, but they had separated; she'd remarried and died soon after. Evelyn wanted me to go upstairs and check, but I was having none of it. My dad mentioned that she wouldn't hurt me, but I've got to say, I did not like going to bed alone from then on and Evelyn left my father soon after.

In 1980, my first job after leaving school was in a warehouse, packing clothing, but the job was boring and the pay was crap. Soon after though, I managed to find work as a tea-boy on a local building site. I was earning good money for my age and was able to start buying things that I'd wanted, like good clothes. It was time to kit out my wardrobe and be able to wear what I wanted to wear.

I bought my first pair of Doc Martins and a pair of combats. Then I went on to build a wardrobe up of Levis, stay pressed trousers, Ben Sherman shirts, Fred Perry T-shirts, a Crombie overcoat, bomber jacket and donkey jacket (not forgetting my Pod shoes). Back in the eighties, it was mainly Punk Rocker, Skinhead, Teddy boy or Mod and the occasional Biker.

I liked the Ska music and the Skinhead clothes, but found the look to be too harsh. I thought it was because of cropped hair that I wasn't lucky with the girls, but in hindsight I see it was my issues back then that affected my relationships.

My father met a lot of women, but none ever stayed around long enough to get serious, at least not till he met my stepmother. He then married this woman and went on to have five more children with her. But, I was pushed out of the family by my stepmother.

I was really happy about finally having a baby brother though and had his name tattooed on my arm, just after he was born. There had been difficulties after his birth and I'd been worried that something might happen to him. It was my first tattoo and it was a swift, with a scroll bearing his name underneath. It probably wasn't the best thing I had done, as it is permanent and it isn't good having another man's name put on you, at the best of times!

The job didn't last though and I got sacked for turning up late to a new site that was out of town. I enjoyed earning money because it meant I could get things that I liked, like nice clothes. For years I had to wear winkle pickers (a slip on shoe with pointed toes) and hand-me-downs.

After leaving school, I progressed to harder drugs and found that I could now get served in the off license at The Green Dragon public house. My drinking had increased since starting as a tea boy on a site where a group of Irish navvies would take me in there during our lunch break and I'd feel like one of the boys. I thought it was big to drink and it made me feel like a man.

CHAPTER SIX

Love Hurts

Most of my teenage years were spent drinking and taking drugs in the local park and the woods surrounding it. There was a group of us, which consisted of old school friends and some new acquaintances; and, one of those was an old neighbour of mine.

I didn't recognise her when I first saw her, as she wasn't the little girl that I'd remembered and these were the people that I'd grown up and gone to school with.

A few of us were at the swing park and I'd climbed up a tree. Looking down, I noticed a couple of girls, but one was looking particularly lovely and made my heart beat faster – it was Ali and she had breasts. Chris had noticed her too and they started seeing each other, so I kept my feelings to myself and put on a brave face.

I'd started experimenting with other new drugs by now. I enjoyed the exhilarating feeling that they gave, but I had to try and conceal any signs of being intoxicated or under the influence of whatever I may have taken. Most, if not all the time, this wasn't hard because my father didn't even notice, now that he had a new family; it was like I was invisible. At least that's what my head might have been telling me, as I tripped out on magic mushrooms, combined with the solvents that I was still sniffing.

The woods and my new friends became my family. We didn't mean any harm; how does that old song go:

"Man, we were killing time, we were young and restless, we just needed to unwind - I knew nothing could last forever." (Bryan Adams – Summer of '69)

But the people walking their dogs in the woods would notice us and feel intimidated and then call the police. It became a game of cat and mouse, when the old bill would turn up and we would all split up and run off in different directions because they couldn't chase all of us.

My offending behaviour started to get out of control and I actually thought that what I was doing was okay. I made excuse after excuse for my behaviour, in and out of court. Since my early conviction for shoplifting, I had taken up stealing on a regular basis; if I wanted something I stole it and always made an excuse to justify my behaviour. It wasn't just these offences getting me in trouble with the police though; because of my drunken behaviour, I was constantly up in front of the local magistrate on charges of criminal damage and other antisocial behaviour.

I was collecting convictions as if they were trophies to be displayed, but without the honourable admiration that they may draw to you; however, a defence barrister who once represented me said that I 'had accrued a somewhat impressive record, in a somewhat depressive manner.' I actually received a community penalty on that occasion because the judge gave me merit for selfless bravery. (But that's for later in my story.)

I left home at seventeen and started sleeping rough, mainly sofa surfing. I use to stay over at Chris and Paul's. They lived with their dad in a flat upstairs, on the second floor to my father. I'd have to sleep under one of their beds, so as not to get caught out by their dad when he came home from the pub. Chris had got quite a name for himself because of his aggression and he had a reputation for not being afraid to use a knife. I had worked with him, labouring for another one of our neighbours, who ran a roofing company. We became close friends and decided to leave home together.

After leaving home, Chris had got himself involved with a guy called Graham, who had just come out of prison and had a long list of convictions, including burglary. He was quite a domineering figure and seemed to have a hold on Chris. We stayed with him and his partner, Christine, for a short time and Chris would go off out late at night with the pair of them, while I stayed behind. Their flat was a foul, dingy place, which appeared to be crawling with grime and slime. I use to sleep in an armchair, fully dressed, with my Crombie wrapped tightly around me, not wanting to come into contact with any infestation that might have been taking place.

One night as I was trying to get some sleep, I heard the front door open and the sound of voices filled the hall. I kept very still, making out that I was asleep, but through the slits of my eyes, I could see an assortment of valuables being placed on the floor. After emptying their coats and pockets, Christine went out in the kitchen to make a cup of tea and I heard Graham say to Chris, "If Mark is staying; he has to pull his weight too".

The next morning, Chris repeated it to me and Graham was more of his intimidating self. Not realising or accepting that I had a choice, I felt obliged - if I wanted to continue having somewhere to stay. So that night, I was taken out on my first job and the feeling was exhilarating, as the adrenaline produced by my fear raced through my body.

We walked around in the dark, looking for somewhere that had easy access because of lack of security or even carelessness. Graham spotted just what he had been looking for and ordered Chris to climb up on the ledge of a first floor flat and gain entry through a window that had been left open. This prevented any glass from being smashed and the occupier from being alerted to an intruder. All Chris had to do was climb in, open the front door and let us in to ransack the house, while the occupants slept undisturbed.

Christine waited outside as a lookout, while the three of us climbed the stairs leading to the flat. There was a hall, with rooms off it to the left and the right. We took a room each and proceeded to search for any valuables and my heart was beating louder than I'd ever known it to. I opened the door in front of me and noticed a double bed beneath a window. In the moonlight, I could see the silhouettes of two lone figures and I drew in a sharp intake of breath. Not only was this home occupied, but they were there, right in front of me. I panicked and turned about to make a quick exit. I grabbed Chris on the way out and said, "They're in, mate!"

We high-tailed it out of the front door as I heard the shout of an alarmed man woken from his slumber. Graham wasn't impressed and the night wasn't over, until finding another property to burgle and making off with the proceeds.

The next day was spent looking for a 'fence' to buy our stolen goods. A fence is someone who buys, receives and sells stolen goods, but there was always somebody who was willing to buy knocked off items, that came at a much-reduced cost than the usual price.

Chris and I would then go to the Green Dragon, which was our local, and get more Dutch courage for the nights that were ahead of us. This pub was notorious for the many characters that frequented it and it became infamous for the Friday and Saturday night brawls that took place among those that entered it. Amongst the people that used it, were a particularly ruthless family, that were known for their aggression and violence and I had run-ins with mostly all of them.

One night, Chris and I were having a pint and a game of pool, when last orders were called. The second oldest of the brothers, named *Dougie*, approached me and said, "Drink up, or I'm taking it off you." Chris was looking at me for my response and, not wanting to lose face, I said, "You'll have to take it off me then." He hesitated for an instant and then said, "I like you – you remind me of me." I'm not sure that was a compliment because he wasn't called 'Dug the Thug' for no reason. But I was starting to find a confidence that was fuelled by drink and propelled by fear.

It wasn't long before the police caught up with me again and I found myself standing in the dock of Portsmouth Crown Court, charged with Burglary x3. Alongside me, were Graham, Christine and Chris and each of us were being represented by a barrister. The charges were read and the prosecutor detailed the events on the nights the offences were committed. Our defence team then did their best to implement mitigating circumstances. Previous convictions reduce the likelihood of mitigation because it produces the fact of likely intent to commit the crime. Graham, Christine and Chris were all sentenced to imprisonment and I escaped with a probation order. They were taken down and I was released and Chris asked me to look after Ali. On another occasion, he had mentioned that if I 'shit' on him, he would hurt me, but I had no intention of doing that, he was my mate.

In a sense, life went back to normal, and I visited my friends at the park. There was a tight bunch of us who became inseparable for a while and Ali was one of them. I used to walk her home at the end of the night and then ride back to the guesthouse that I was staying in at Pompey.

My Uncle Cyril had acted as guarantor, so that I could purchase a motorbike on finance. Ali hadn't mentioned Chris for a while and I had become very fond of her because of her sweet and soft nature. I asked her what the score was with her and Chris. She convinced me that it was nothing serious and I left it at that. I used to go round her mum's for a cup of tea and one time she was looking at some picture cards on the table. I asked her what they were and she told me they were tarot cards and asked if I'd like her to do me a reading. Intrigued, I agreed and some cards were dealt before me. She turned a card over and laughed, so I asked her what was funny. There was a couple in an intimate embrace and it suggested that we might be lovers. I felt a surge of excitement, as I'd been attracted to her for some time, but I pursued it no further because I wasn't sure.

It came to me whilst riding my motorbike home one evening that maybe I should turn back and ask her if she was interested in me. I pulled up outside her house and threw stones up at her window, to get her attention. I saw a curtain go back and I felt nervous, as the window opened. "Hi yaw, what's up?" she said.

"Will you go out with me?" I asked.

She said yes and that was that. Ali was now my girlfriend and I rode home content that night, looking forward to seeing her the next day.

Ali was more experienced than I, as I hadn't gone further than the occasional clumsy fumble. My friend Kevin commented on me taking it further and one evening, after a couple of beers, we were allowed to use his bedroom. That first time was awkward and embarrassing, but now I had got laid with a girl and I thought that I was in love. I was deceived; I even had her name tattooed across my heart. But, I wasn't mature enough to understand the fundamentals in a relationship, like caring and showing affection; I was only interested in the physical side.

The coupled liaison that we had was short- lived and not because of any interest that I might have shown in another girl; but because I realised Ali hadn't quite been honest about her relationship with Chris, and his brother Paul had predicted trouble when he got out. We finished and another girl called Wendy comforted me after our separation.

Chris came out of detention centre and got back with Ali. We had a set to, and I'd been prepared for a 'straightener', but Chris wasn't prepared to fight me 'ma-no a ma-no'. He walked into the Green Dragon one night and offered me 'outside', to which I willingly complied. He then said, "Not here, up the park," and so I followed him across the road and down a path, that went through the nearby woods. He stopped suddenly by a tree and took out two knives. He offered me one of them, but I refused to fight him with it. I didn't see what warranted us hurting each other so badly, never mind killing him.

We talked and I could see that Chris believed that I'd mugged him off, but that was just his opinion, having only ever heard Ali's side of the story. I refused to give my version as I wasn't trying to pass any blame, but I was wondering what my part had been in all this; apart from having liked her for a very long time. I thought that we'd put it behind us and would often accompany them on nights out, but I didn't always have a date for myself.

We were playing pool in a pub one night and Chris got up to go to the toilet. Ali started asking me if I remembered the stuff that we used to do and I told her to leave it out, as she was with Chris now. At the end of the night we went back to a house that they were staying in. After a short argument, Ali went off to bed and Chris and I started to drink some wine. Later on, he went to bed and left me to sleep on the sofa. I'd heard them arguing earlier, but hadn't known what it was about, until I woke up with a sharp pain in one side of my back and Chris looming over me. He was shouting, as he lunged at me again and I had to kick him to get him off me. He then started crying, but I was aware of a warm wet trickling down my back and it hurt when I breathed. Ali came downstairs and Chris shouted at her to find something to stop the blood. I then realised I'd been stabbed, but my only concern was not to cause a panic. Someone mentioned getting an ambulance, but I assured them that I was fine and would go to the doctor's surgery in the morning. Ali stayed up to bathe the wounds and Chris went to bed.

The next day, after an appointment with the local doctor, I was admitted to hospital. I was very lucky, as the stab wound in my back had just missed my lung. Chris had come with me in the taxi, and now sat by my bedside. Somehow, my mum's brother had got wind of it and I now had a visit from my Uncle Derek, asking me, "Who did it?"

I could hear the anger in his tone and I wasn't convinced that it would be a good idea telling him; besides, I'd decided that I had to fight my own battles, although it was cowardly to stab a man in the back, never mind while he was sleeping. I lied about not knowing who did it and after that my uncle left it. I mentioned to Chris something like: "It's something I won't forget, but I'll try to forgive you, as long as I'm not made to remember it!"

CHAPTER SEVEN

Fighting the System

In 1982, I started to do my own thing and moved into a quiet guesthouse in the town. I'd have to be out during the day and was allowed back after five. I had my own room at the top of the three-storey building and was provided with a cooked breakfast every morning. It was just a roof over my head, which I considered temporary, until better things came along.

One morning, I was rushing to finish the fry up that was before me. I was in a hurry. As I bounced out of the dining room, I bumped into a fit looking brunette that had a warm, welcoming smile and so I decided that I needed another coffee. Roy, the landlord, was rather more attentive to this mystery girl than all the other guests, including me. I noticed that he'd placed an extra sausage on her plate and it made me laugh. I finished my drink and got up from the table and went out.

Later that evening, I came back and heard the sound of a TV in the room below me. I had nothing better to do so I knocked the door, with the intention of introducing myself to my new neighbour. The door opened and standing inside the room was the girl from breakfast and she invited me in. She introduced herself as Shelley and she said that she was waiting for a move to her own council place for her and her young son, Darren. We hit it off straight away and she told me how the landlord had made unwanted advances at her. We stayed up together that night, talking, watching telly and having a laugh.

The next morning we went down for breakfast and sat at the same table. Roy was not impressed with our obvious attraction, which meant she didn't get an extra sausage from him and I was asked to leave the very next day.

I moved around from one B&B to another after that and there was nothing else to do in those places, except get smashed. Most people were out of work and I hadn't been able to keep a job either. I was a thief and stealing had become my vocation in life.

My offending continued and it wasn't long before I found myself being arrested again and charged with thefts and more burglaries. This time there was no probation or any community penalty and I was sentenced to six months in a detention centre – a short sharp shock, or so they called it!

Erlestoke Detention Centre in Devizes was a place that they sent you to shake you up and sort you out. It was ruled by discipline and order, involving military-type training and a bunch of prison officers with attitude.

Crime surely doesn't pay and karma is a bastard. It was now time for me to pay for a mistake that I made all those years ago, back in the junior school, of trapping a little girl's finger in the door. Her father, the bobby, had a job down at the local nick and he was 'Dick the Jailer'. He got the job of escorting me to my new home. In reception, Dick made a remark to one of the officers standing nearby. "You've got a right one here," he said. I'm sure it wasn't meant to make my stay there any easier!

Things got tougher from then on and I had my face smashed against the wall, as this burly screw reminded me who was boss. After induction, I was taken down to the house-block, which consisted of a two-floor block of cells.

I could almost smell the fear of those that had been taken out of their own safe environment and placed in a hostile one, full of adversity.

Everyone looked forward to the day's post, hoping that a loved one would remind them that they still had something to look forward to - unless you were unfortunate enough to be told by the missus that she didn't love you anymore and had found someone else; then it would really kick off. This is what's known as a 'Dear John'. Weekends were for visits; they were only once a fortnight provided that your family or partner could get there to see you.

Shelley wrote regularly and I enjoyed her letters because they were warm and encouraging. I'd intended to make a go of it with her and Darren on my release. I had an appeal lodged against the sentence and was waiting for my court hearing.

I wasn't looking for any trouble but it found me, in the shape of a prison bully who was attempting to intimidate and control me and others. I'd had it with bullies and I wasn't going to back down; besides in prison you can't walk away because there's no place to run.

In the evenings, depending on which landing you were on, there was association. It's a chance to have a shower, go to gym, watch telly or go into the games room, but you don't get to do it all. It's also the time that those who are drug dependent run around looking to see if anyone has any pot or the likes. Detention centres weren't known for the availability of any substances because security and control measures were much more stringent. This meant that the fit young offender, who was filled up on adrenaline- fuelled testosterone, would not always express themselves in a likeable manner. On one or two occasions, I had a run in with these individuals. A black boy accosted me on the way upstairs to the television room one evening. He came across very aggressively and threatened violence. But it was over before it began and it just resulted in him cussing me under his breath. This is the usual scenario, although, if you show any fear, it can escalate into a further threat or risk of harm.

There are those inside who use any kind of force to manipulate you into submission and violence is their most effective tool. There's a hierarchy, with the big man at the top and the smaller men at the bottom; but bullies are just small men wanting to appear big. I stood up to them, whether they were inmate or screw and it cost me a lot of time in solitary. On one occasion, a group of us on Induction were marching around a basketball court, which had been designated as our parade ground. The officer that was barking out the orders suddenly turned on this little guy and started to give him a really hard time. I told him to pick on someone his own size and when he turned and demanded what was said, you could have heard a pin drop. As I mentioned earlier, discipline was tight and no one wanted to be on the receiving end of these militant oppressors. Except, silly bugger me, who didn't know when to keep his mouth shut and I piped up: "You heard me!" Everyone was marched back in and I was made to grab all my kit and then double-marched over to the block-house.

During my time down the 'block', I faced my father again and again, shouting at me and telling me what to do. Of course, the governor was just a representation of all that I hated about authority. I'd had enough of it and shouted back at him, "F--- off, you c---."

The prison system tried to get into arbitrary talks with my parents, because I was out of control and respected no authority. I was told by a housemaster that I had transgressed and I was charged with insubordination and being truculent. I didn't have a clue what they were on about and just thought that they could stick it up their ass.

I actually had liked Shelley; she was a bright and beautiful girl with a good head on her shoulders - but I didn't feel quite good enough for her. What I mean is, she was open with her emotions and showed her love freely.

I, on the other hand, had become hostile and offensive. Too much time in solitary confinement can do that to any person and I'd just spent the last three months down the block, wrapped up inside my own head.

My heart had hardened in the time that I'd been away and I didn't go back to her. When I was released, I had no intention of settling down. I thought that the world owed me something and I was going to take it.

About this time, just after my release, I visited the Job Centre, to see if there might be any job prospects. Whilst standing and viewing the latest vacancies, I noticed someone familiar, standing just a few feet away. My heart started to beat faster, as I recognised the face before me. It was the *nonce* (the guy who had approached me when I was a kid in the woods) and I thought quickly of what to say. I asked him what he was doing there and he replied that he was looking for a job. I then asked what kind of job and he replied: "An electrician." I became angry and accused him of not being an electrician but a sex-case and I head-butted him, right there in the Job Centre. He threatened to get the police and I retorted: "What are you going to do, go in there and say that you tried to nonce a 12-year old kid and unfortunately he's come back and done you?" His face went white when he realised who I was and he quickly left. I had further run-ins with him and he came off worse each time. I even kicked him off his cycle as I rode past him on my motorbike. I saw him in a shopping precinct one time, when I was out with one of my girlfriends. He walked past me as we were walking along, hand in hand. She was walking alongside me, holding my left hand and I hit him with my right one. He hit the ground and when she asked me what had happened, I lied and said he must have had a fit. I'm not sure if she believed me, but I didn't see him again after that. I make no excuse for my behaviour then; I had been afraid for myself and for any other child that may have been a victim of this man.

A few months later I received another custodial sentence, with four months and a day, to be served in a youth custody centre. First of all I was sent up to H.M.P. Winchester, in the Y.O.P. section called 'The Dolls' House'. Then I was allocated to Guys Marsh youth custody centre. This was a semi-open nick, although I could have walked right out the gate, if I'd been of a mind.

During Induction I met the governor, who had been nicknamed 'Rat Face' by someone who obviously hadn't enjoyed the hospitality there. The governor mentioned to me that if looks could kill, then he would have been dead. I replied that there was still time and anything could happen. I've got to say, that man was harsh, but fair. I often found myself in front of him on adjudication, down the block answering to a breach of rules or other offences, such as fighting. The standard procedure was being escorted off the wing, or in this case, dormitory, with force if necessary. Restraints are available for more violent prisoners, such as CNR (control and restraint), which is not meant for comfort and if you struggle – it hurts!

The offender is then placed in a cell in the segregation unit and isolated if he poses a threat to another inmate or prison officer. Normally, the next day, the prison governor is called to the block and a small courtroom is set aside for him to hear each individual case. He is seated one end of the room behind a table, with an officer each side of him and the offender is brought in and made to sit behind a table at the other end of the room with a guard on each side of him. The officer who has placed the inmate on 'report' reads out the charge and the offender offers a plea. The difference between that and a hearing in court is, the case of the defendant is often weakened and punishment is guaranteed. I often had the experience of falling foul of a particularly nasty screw and losing my status and loss of privileges. There are different regimes in different nicks, but an enhanced status can be earned which will get you extra visits, an X box and more spends in the canteen, although you do have to have the funds in your private cash to do so.

I had a low tolerance and was often immobilized by frustration and anger towards idiots that ran away with their mouths or gave it large, making out that they were something that they were not and, more often than not, at the expense of someone else, in this case – me!

I was in the wing office one morning, checking if I had any mail and, finding out that I had none, I tried to leave. Another inmate called Jarvis stood in my way and I asked him politely to move. He took my courtesy as weakness and remained in the way, so I pushed through him. As I walked away he made some derogatory remark, loud enough for everyone to hear, including me. It was a challenge, but I didn't react on this occasion. I went to my room and did some press-ups to let off some steam. He continued to aggravate me until, on one occasion; I caught him in the boot-room alone. I asked him if he wanted to make something of it and some shouting took place, which alerted the screws. He didn't want to know until the 'cavalry' arrived and went for me. I retaliated with a punch to his head, which knocked him backwards and the two screws present lunged at me and took me down the block.

Next morning, I was up in front of Rat Face and he gave me 'time' down the block, with no loss of remission (earliest date of release not affected). The governor has the power to extend your period of custody from your E.D.R. - L.D.R. When receiving a sentence an inmate is usually released earlier than the actual finishing date. It's normally the half way mark (up to 4 years) and then it's two thirds of the sentence to be spent in custody and the rest in the community, on license.

To be honest, spending time in solitary or being banged up behind a door, wasn't a problem for me – I prefer my own company. I would serve my time down the block, and then be returned to the dorm, having lost my room, which was a privilege that had to be earned. The dorms were hostile places for the unlearned and the vulnerable.

On the very first night there, a ginger guy from Plymouth had been entertaining an entourage that followed him out of fear, when one of the guys that came in with me told him to belt up. It was lights out, late and we all wanted to get our 'nuts' down. This didn't go down too well with the red haired lout and he jumped out of bed and came over our side of the dorm, shouting: "Who f------ said that?" My pal thought it best not to answer and the bully had a go at the man in the bed next to me. I told him to leave him alone and was saved by the night watchman coming round the corner. The guy ran back to his bed and shouted a threat out to me in the dark. It quietened down for the night and I got up and went for my kitchen duty the next morning.

I loved working in the kitchen because it was away from the mainframe of the prison; the guards were more accommodating and there were the perks of enjoying more food, or at least a wider choice.

It had been a busy morning and I was having a five minute break out back by the gate and I heard some taunts coming from outside. My ginger friend was returning from his work duty, ready for lunch, and accompanying him were two others from the dorm. They were taunting me through the Iron Gate bars, about how I was going to get it and that I needed to learn some respect. I would have agreed with that, but not from them. I have to admit though, when they walked off, I could feel the old sphincter muscle twitching and I was full of apprehension about what lay ahead for me.

After work, I was heading back down a long walkway between dorms, when I detected some threat ahead. Still feeling apprehensive, I trod carefully forward. As I approached the next corner I was fully prepared for the attack, which came from my left. I swerved out of the way of a punch that had been thrown and countered with a left hook that sent the assailant reeling. It was my old buddy, *Ginger*, and his two goons, who, on seeing his demise, had done one and legged it. I never got nicked for that one, but it did change the dynamics in the dorm and on the house-block that I was on.

Rat Face was ever the diplomat and used this new status of mine to lure other young offenders to the Christmas Mass in the chapel. He promised me a Mars bar if I went, presuming that I'd tell the others and they would follow suit. The night of the service, I was getting prepared and changing into the kit that was reserved especially for adjudication, church and visits. I noticed a few lads coming back from the service eating chocolate bars. I asked them where they got them and they replied that they were from the chaplain. I had either misheard or the governor, who had led me to believe that I was personally getting the Mars from him, had misled me. So I started to get undressed, back into the regular kit of t-shirt, jeans and trainers. I was lying on my bed reading, when I got an unexpected visit from the governor. Rat Face asked if I was coming to the service and I told him I wasn't because I felt he had mislead me to believe that I was getting something direct from him that everyone else wasn't privy to. He asked me to follow him and led me down the long corridor between the dorms, until we reached the centre, where the canteen was located. He got a prison officer to open it up and he went in and picked up an assortment of chocolate bars from the shelf. He asked me, "Will this do?" and I sheepishly took them and made my way back to my dorm and changed.

I'm so glad that the governor took time out to get me to go to that service because it was a good night, where people came together. There were the inmates from the different dorms and visitors from the community, enjoying festivities and putting differences aside and I loved it – if I'd known better, I might not have even taken the bribe!

These institutions are not holiday camps and I'm not trying to make light of them, because they are tough and you have to have eyes up your ass to stay on your feet. Someone will always try and take you down and then there are those who just think they're 'hard'. Kitchens are volatile places enough; there are plenty of hot spots that can cause danger. Large pots which are called 'coppers' are full of hot stews, soups and the like and alongside them are the steamers that cook joints and boil potatoes before they are mashed. Then, there are the ovens that bake pies, bread, even chicken. These ovens are in the bake-house normally and there are orderlies that assist the cook to prepare all these foods. (I must stress at this point that these institutions are not renowned for their culinary delights.)

In the bake house was an orderly called Travers, who was nicknamed 'Tasty Pastry' because he thought he was the 'mutt's nuts.' Most of us would get on well enough to do our own individual job, but I found him extremely irritating; especially during one afternoon. I was taking a short break and allowing a money spider to walk across my palm as I sat back and rested from a morning's work. Out of nowhere, I felt an unexpected slap across my wrist. I looked down and saw blood where my little insect friend had been beforehand. As I was looking up at the figure looming over me, my friend, Barney, seated beside me said, "Leave it, Shep, he's not worth it!"

Later that afternoon, we were just shutting the hatch to the dining hall and the rest of the inmates were tucking into their grub. I was starving and was in a hurry to eat and then get back to my house-block for a shower. For some reason there was a queue for the butter (little noblets that have been cut to the size of a ration) and the boys in the kitchen were getting slightly irritated. I noticed that old Tasty Pastry was at the front of it, spreading some bread. I could feel myself getting annoyed and said something like: "Come on, Travers, you mug; sort it out!" He wasn't fazed and called back to me a rude name and I took offence. I head-butted him in the back of his head and it must have hurt me more, but he went down like a sack of potatoes. The kitchen screw was aware of a commotion and came round the other side of the kitchen to see old Tasty getting up from the floor, holding his head. I can't remember if I'd been seen or if someone had grassed me up, but I was sacked on the spot and sent back to my wing.

I went to my room and was getting changed out of my 'whites', when I heard the sharp loud sound of hobnail boots, coming down my landing and I knew that I was in the s---!

Two burly block screws swung into my room and ordered me to change into my number ones and then they marched me down to segregation sharply. Placed into a cell, I started to recall events leading up to my recent incarceration.

Before I had been sent down, I had met a lovely girl called Tracy, who was staying with her married sister who lived in the navy quarters. I'd seen her in a park opposite the Green Dragon, just days before I got imprisoned and asked her out. She was fresh faced and had an innocent shyness, unlike the other girls that I had been dating. She had written and visited me and we had planned to share Christmas alone together at her sister's. I hadn't taken any of this into consideration during my time away, but had expected her to be there for me at the end of it!

So, here I was once again, in a cell block, waiting for adjudication because of my rebellious behaviour. The festive season was just round the corner and I was soon to be discharged once again. I'd been looking forward to my release, but for all the wrong reasons. Tracy had stated that she was a virgin and had promised herself to me on my first night out of prison.

It all started to dawn on me, the seriousness of the situation which I was now in, as the cell door opened and the block screw marched me into a waiting office, which represented a minor courtroom. I never really heard the charge being read out or how it had been viewed as a callous attack. The words that echoed around the room were: "three weeks' loss of remission." I heard the air leaving my body as the effect of the sentence registered in my brain. A quick calculation made my new E.D.R. the 31st December. Before I could say anything, I was escorted back to my cell, with the door being slammed behind me. I was choked up and it didn't help matters when the governor, visiting me during his rounds, stated that he had made an error. He insisted that he mistakenly thought that I was to be released on the 3rd and this would have meant I was discharged on Christmas Eve. I had been due to be released on the 10th and I asked if he could change it, hoping that he would say yes. He apologetically stated that it was impossible for him to reverse the decision and I exploded, telling him to f--- off then!

This made a harsh impression on me and I became less interested in setting any good example. However, bribery is an efficient tool to apply any leverage, but not so much more effective than blackmail. My reputation of 'taking no nonsense' hadn't gone unnoticed by those who were managing the young offenders. The chief prison officer had invited me up to his office one afternoon and as I walked in the beckoned me to a chair in front of his large desk. There were no pleasantries in the way of formal greetings, offer of beverages or anything. The chief was a big man and he had something important to say and, as far as he was concerned, it was his nick and I was going to listen.

"Listen to me, Shepard, there have been some isolated incidents of particularly harsh and cruel racism in your dorm and it has to stop!" he barked at me.

After ascertaining that he knew that I wasn't responsible for these incidents, he subtly implied that unless it was stopped, everyone would be held responsible and Christmas would not be as good as it could be in one of her majesty's institutions. He also stated that I was a lad of reputation and that he wanted me to use my influence to put a stop to it. On any other occasion, I might have told him to 'do one', but I only had a few weeks left myself and decided that I would look into it.

During that night, I was just dropping off to sleep, when a couple of lads got out of their bunks and crept over to the bed of a black boy. It was common for the boys to tip each other out of their beds to amuse each other. As I looked over, I noticed that one of the lads had a roll-up in his mouth, which he took out and was just about to put it out on a boy who lay asleep, unaware of any threat. "Behave!" I snarled at the perpetrator. He stopped in his tracks, but said: "Leave it out; he's only a black b-----d." I went to swing myself out of bed and replied, "If you touch him one more time, I'll f----- have you." Both lads had a change of mind and that was the end of that.

Christmas soon passed, but not before I won a writing competition for a verse that I wrote called 'Christmas Time'. I won a bag of strawberry truffles for that, but the achievement was far greater than any prize.

That reminds me of a sales competition that I was entered into, back when I first left school, in one of Curry's electrical stores. I was sixteen and impressionable and was keen to prove myself as a salesman. There were about five other senior sales persons and a manager that I was up against, but I came out clearly in front. However, first position was given to the person behind me in second place because I was on a youth opportunity program. This wasn't discussed in the first instance and I was angry at the decision. I justified it by stealing from the company on numerous occasions. I would pick the lock of a glass case that held watches, calculators and other small gadgets. I once went home with three watches on my wrists, which were sold in a pub later that evening. I also put additions on the delivery sheet, which was a way to smuggle stolen goods out of the back of the store. I was eventually fired though, for giving away a head cleaner to a customer who had just bought a stereo cassette player.

I served three sentences in youth custody and none of them acted as a deterrent.

CHAPTER EIGHT

In Too Deep

In 1984, I was twenty-one years old and miles away from where I considered home. After coming out of youth custody, I had tried to make a go of it up in North Wales with my mum and sisters. I'd managed to get a small bedsit in some holiday flats, after a short spell at Kate's.

My mum had been proud at first to show off her newfound son. I went to the leisure centre that she worked at as a receptionist, to do a workout. During my time away, I had hit the gym and had developed a good habit of keeping strong and fit. As a result, I had good muscle tone and my fitness levels were very good.

Whilst I was in the weight room, one of the female instructors left the room and went to the reception. She made a comment to the girls on the desk about a certain young man who was working out. My mum overheard and her colleague told her to tell the girl who I was. On that occasion my mum was pleased to mention about having me around.

I managed to secure two jobs, working both during the day (in construction, on a new carriageway that was being built) and in the evening as a barman.

Life was generally good. I had my family, my flat, my job and money to spend. I worked hard, but played harder and liked to have a drink at the end of the day. I don't really know what happened, but somewhere along the way, my drinking got out of hand. I wasn't drinking on a social basis; I drank to get completely smashed.

One of the perks of working in bars in a seaside resort is the girls and another is free entry into clubs after hours. I got drunk regularly after work and thought nothing of it, or the reckless behavior that came with it.

On one occasion, I was on my way home after a night out. I used to stop off at a KFC and one of the girls there would sort me out with the odd free bargain bucket of chicken. I would take some back for a kitten that I shared my flat let with. I stopped to relieve myself and a building caught my attention. I booted open the front door, made of solid wood, and made my way into an office. I searched through some filing cabinets and eventually came across two cash boxes. I then made a sharp exit and shot off down the street, which was literally 1000 yards up the road from my place. I went around the back of the flat lets to a cellar that was beneath my room. I found a hammer and smashed open the tins and emptied the contents. There was £630 in cash and I felt well made up with the result.

The next morning, I went to see my mum and asked her if she could look after a wad of notes for me. She wasn't impressed and was also worried that I might be caught for breaking into the premises. I assured her it would be fine and told her to get her hair done because we were going out. That evening I took my mum out for a nice meal, but she hardly ate a thing; instead she wanted a Kentucky on the way home.

I never seemed to have enough money; no matter how much I had, it never lasted long enough to invest in something worthwhile and planning for my future wasn't an idea that I entertained. I stole whatever I wanted and never thought of the consequences - to me or my family.

The final straw for my mum was my being arrested for a couple of break-ins in the town. My mum was a hard worker and sometimes held a couple of jobs at the same time. She was respected in her community and her wayward son turning up and creating havoc was more than she could handle.

I was charged with two offences of burglary (commercial) and remanded for a period in HMP Risley in Cheshire. I had broken into a baker's shop for something to eat. I'd been out for the night drinking and had left it too late to get any food from a take-away because they were all closed. Whilst walking past the baker's, I had clocked a cabinet full of pies, pizza and cake and the temptation was too great. I smashed a door and entered. As I sat on the counter helping myself I heard the sound of a police radio, acknowledging their presence at the premises. I was too intoxicated to get away.

I didn't see my drinking as a problem, but then again I had hidden from my problems through drink. My twenty-first birthday came round; I was now unemployed, bored and feeling far from a place called home. I went to the pub to celebrate and drank alone. It was miserable and I soon ran out of money so I left. I headed off back to my pokey flat, but something caught my attention.

I broke into a closed butcher's shop because I'd been attracted to the sales light on the cash register. Unfortunately, the owner was still on the premises and observed me leaving the building and crossing the road to a phone box. I was on the phone to my dad, telling him how unhappy I was up in Wales, when the police arrived and arrested me.

I spent a couple of weeks on remand before going to court and being sentenced. There weren't so many restrictions back then and those on remind were entitled to have food brought in by their visitors. My mum was kind enough to bring me some goodies but, nevertheless, I was a bit agitated because my mum was a good dresser and she had shopped at M&S. This wasn't the typical stereotype of a normal offender and I felt as if I stood out; I did appreciate the good grub though.

This all went in my favor at court, as the bench had heard that my mum was of impeccable character and that I'd been a troubled youth, just trying to find my way. I thought I'd had another result, until I decided to go down to Gosport for the weekend to see my uncle and my mum decided that I'd be better off back down there. She sent my suitcases down on a train behind me and I had to collect them from 'Lost Property' the following day.

My mum might have been prepared to give me another chance, if the local paper hadn't printed an exclusive of something along the lines of: 'A hoodlum from down south arrives in sunny seaside town and let's loose, creating havoc and mayhem for local shopkeepers'.

So my mum stopped being so keen to have me around after that and the irony of it is that the write-up in the paper was printed by a similar small business to the ones that I'd broken into without any regard.

That should have been a lesson to me and even a wakeup call, but I just continued to drink and block it out. I didn't want to listen to anybody except myself and I thought I knew what was best for me.

To tell you the truth, I wasn't impressed with the way things were turning out. Twenty-one years old and what did I have to show for it? I longed to make something of myself and bring honor back to the family name, which I felt had been dishonored by me and my father.

I thought it might be good to go into the armed services, as I felt that I had plenty to fight for. I decided to visit the army careers office and was booked in for an interview shortly afterwards. I then had to sit an exam, before taking a medical. I received high marks in my written test and the interviewing officer commented on the fact that, as a result of getting good grades, I could choose whichever regiment I wanted to enlist in. I was even offered a place in the intelligence corps, but I insisted that I wanted to fight and not to learn. After passing the medical and having one last interview, I was told that I would be sent my selection papers and a train warrant for Sutton Coldfield, near Birmingham.

The day my papers came, I opened the letter and saw that I had been selected for the 2nd Parachute Regiment and I felt awesome. I began some physical training to prepare myself for the selection tests. I would run each day and finish with some pull-ups at a local park to build up upper body strength.

Just before I was due to travel up north to the army camp, I was drinking in one of my local pubs and I got talking to a guy who had just come back from the same training camp. I asked him how he'd done and he told me how he had lied during his application and had been kicked out, with the possibility of a large fine.

This was like a bad omen to me because during my first interview, when I'd been asked if I had any criminal convictions, I had omitted any serious ones like burglary. I felt that I would be found out too and didn't fancy the embarrassment of being asked to leave or the feelings of rejection that came with it.

I did actually have it confirmed by an army recruitment officer that I would have been deselected because of unspent convictions. He also mentioned that it was their loss, but it was no consolation to me.

This was a huge blow to my confidence and I resigned myself to the fact that my record would define my future.

So my life consisted of beer, girls and stealing to fund my way of living. I burgled houses, shops and any other premises that might be holding cash or the valuables to obtain it. I wasn't even concerned with being caught or going to prison, in fact that just made it more interesting, getting one over on the old bill.

I spent a lot of time with my uncle, a lovable rogue, who had the respect of those in our community. I looked up to him and would listen to his advice, but wasn't inclined to taking any. I'm not proud to admit this, but I even stole from him.

He used to let me borrow his clothes and, going through his wardrobe one day, I came across a wad of notes. I thought that he wouldn't miss a ten-pound note or even a score and I helped myself.

He used to have a few mates around, who were well known local faces and one of the men was a man that I looked up to, called Jimmy.

He was quite a lad and his brothers were well known in the Gosport area too. I admired and respected him and heard some stories of what they had all been up to, but I saw Jimmy as the brightest button. He and my uncle both took me under their wing. They both tried to encourage me not to take the crooked path, but I wasn't listening and I aspired to be just like these two men that I admired.

I loved spending time in their company and it made me feel like one of the lads. The only time I didn't go to the pub, was when we all used to get together around my uncle's and have a lads' night in. This would consist of smoking some dope, playing crib or some other card game and having a laugh.

A trip to France was arranged and I asked if I could go with them. On the morning before setting off, I arrived around my uncle's and went into his kitchen. A couple of the lads were snorting some white powder off a mirror and I asked if I could have some. They weren't too happy because they were concerned about what my uncle might say, but I was eventually allowed to try some. I didn't feel the effect until we were on board the ferry.

I suddenly felt this great surge of energy and the need to do something physical; I just couldn't sit still. My uncle looked at me suspiciously, but his suspicions weren't aroused any further until one of the ship's company reported to him that the young fellow travelling with them was running around the above deck.

He came to find me and I was dragged back downstairs and told to hold it down. We played cards as the ferry sailed across the English Channel and drank a couple of litres of spirit. At some stage I needed to use the toilets and, whilst standing in the gents, I looked down at my member. I was alarmed to see that it had not only shrunk, but shriveled up to just its foreskin. I panicked and asked my uncle if this was a permanent condition. He held a straight face and replied yes. I was wounded, until suddenly they all burst out laughing. I was too relieved to feel embarrassed.

The following day, after we got back, I developed a severe rash all over my body and had to go to the doctor's. I told the G.P that I'd used speed and asked whether it could have caused it. He asked me if I'd used anything else. I assured him that I hadn't, except the drink, and told him how much I had drunk. I was then told that I was having a reaction, due to alcohol poisoning.

So I didn't drink again, at least for a couple of days, and thought at least it wasn't the drugs. I believed that I was just a recreational user and that would be how it would stay.

I did like to spend a lot of time down the pub and that would cost a lot of money, which meant that I was always looking for a way to fund it.

The burglaries that I committed were quick smash and grabs. Even when I broke into a house, I would make my way to the front room and see if there was a video player, as I could get £100 for a good name brand like Ferguson. I would then put it by the front door and check to see if there was an electric meter, as I was able to remove this quickly by removing two small screws, which attached it to the unit. These meters would hold up to a couple of hundred pounds, but mostly I'd get £100 out of them too. I would smash them open and dump the empty boxes. As far as I was concerned, I wasn't taking anything personal or something that couldn't be replaced.

I would then go to one of my regular bars to drink the proceeds. On one occasion, whilst in the gents of a local town inn, I clocked a small window that I believed I could gain access to. I left the pub and went and got a hacksaw and screwdriver.

Going back to the pub, I went straight back to the toilets, undid the screws that were holding two metal strips across the window and sawed off the ends. I then replaced them, opened the window and pulled it to, with an elastic band to hold it in place, giving the appearance that it was shut. I then left the bar and visited my uncle.

The American Super bowl was on that night and I watched the Chicago Bulls win the game, before leaving to go and case the bar. It was late and the town had closed. I sneaked around the back of the pub and opened the window. I then moved to a safe place to see if I'd created a disturbance. Seeing it was all clear, I returned and gained entry. I went into the bar and started on opening the front of a fruit machine. The tray was full and I started to empty it, thinking I'd try the cellar next. I had heard that the manager put the takings in there at night.

Suddenly, I noticed a moving shadow through the curtains and took a peep. Outside the head barman was checking the doors with a lit torch in his hand. I kept perfectly still, hoping that with no obvious signs of a break-in, he might disappear. I forgot to close the window that I had gained entry by and shortly after there were headlights outside, with the full beam shining straight through the long pane of glass facing the High Street.

I looked for somewhere to hide and the only place available to me was behind a tabletop space invader. As I got onto my knees behind it, the lounge door was opened and in ran some boys in blue. They proceeded straight to the toilets and I thought this would be my chance for a quick getaway. I stood up and made for the door, but one of the coppers had turned round. He shouted and raised the alarm to get further assistance, which was waiting outside the door. I could not avoid running straight into the arms of the law.

I was arrested and taken down to the cells to wait for my interview.

I would like to think that on this occasion it had just been a case of bad luck, but I don't think I was a particularly clever burglar as shortly before this I had broken into a florist's one night, after again meticulously planning an elaborate break-in. On the evening in question, I had left my room in a bed-and- breakfast in Pompey. I was dressed in black for the occasion. I had taken great care to empty all my pockets and leave my belongings behind. I caught the ferry to Gosport and made my way to one of the shops along the High Street. I managed to gain entry round the back of the shop, climbing in through a smashed window. I then grabbed what little was available because the sharp shop owner had been smarter than me, locking all cash away in a concealed and secure lock up. Having nothing to gain, I left the premises and made way back home. Shortly after, I was picked up by Gosport CID and taken in for questioning. I sat in the interview room all smug, thinking that they wouldn't get anything out of me. I would usually say: 'No comment', unless it was serious and then I would answer their questions, making a statement but omitting anything that would incriminate me or others.

Normally, I would have some satisfaction in seeing the interviewing officer go red in the face as I wormed my way out of the allegations. Bu the only face that was going red in this interview was mine. DC Ashton was trying not to smile as he asked me:

"Did you break into Auto Flora on such and such night?"

My reply: "No."

"Are you sure?"

"Course I am," I grinned sheepishly.

"Can you tell me how this managed to travel across the harbor on a ferry, make its way up the High Street and round the back of and through the window of the said shop, finally resting itself in a sink by the back window?" He grinned back as he held up a railcard with my boat race on it.

I was charged with Burglary x2, and committed to Portsmouth Crown Court to await sentencing. I was playing with the big boys now and my time in youth custody was over. This was my first taste of main prison and I received two years' imprisonment.

CHAPTER NINE

Big Time Now

HMP Winchester is on top of a hill and from my cell window on the '4s' landing; I could survey the surrounding countryside and enjoy a great view. I'd look out of it at the miniscule cars driving down some road, which cut through the Twyford Down. I used to remind myself that I'd be out there soon, being free to go where I liked.

All my family, except my uncle and Aunty Sylv, seemed to have deserted me (who could blame them). I suddenly found myself very alone and in isolation (literally). I spent more time in solitary confinement than up on the wing.

On Sundays there was chapel; it was a good place to catch up with a friendly face or, even better, to get some burn. A lot of the inmates went there to get out of their cells or just to do a deal and I was no different.

I didn't particularly enjoy the services, but that might have been because it was hard taking anything in and believing it. The chaplain would often talk about a loving God and a man named Jesus, who came not to break the law, but to fulfill it.

After the service, there would be tea and coffee and a chance to talk to the chaplaincy team. This was an opportunity for the inmates to ask the chaplain any questions and most were about getting a telephone call home to a loved one. There was also a bookshelf at the back of the chapel and alongside Bibles in different translations, were books with titles such as: 'Run, Baby, Run', 'The Cross and the Switchblade', 'Hell's Angel' and 'Chasing the Dragon'.

I read them all and they each carried a story of redemption. I enjoyed the testimonies but didn't see myself, in any shape or form, fitting the description of someone that could be made good...

HMP Winchester is only a short-term nick and they usually allocate inmates after categorization. This can depend on several factors: seriousness of offence, previous convictions and behavior whilst in custody.

As I wasn't a model prisoner, I was transferred to HMP Dartmoor, a prison located deep in the moors down in Devon. As you approach the main gate, above it is an inscription in Latin, which reads:

'Abandon all hope, ye that enter here.'

Dartmoor Prison was originally built at Prince town in Devon between 1806 and 1809 to house French captives during the Napoleonic Wars. During the War of 1812 many American prisoners were also confined there.

The coach that was transporting a bunch of criminals waited for the gatekeeper to swing wide the ancient gates and we entered our newfound home.

The prison is placed at the heart of a barren landscape, with a cloud that perpetually hangs over it. The walls are a dismal grey and so is the countenance of those that reside there.

We were all taken to reception, to wait for which wing we would be allocated to. I looked around at the group that I was in and could see how harrowing it was for most of us. It can be quite daunting, finding your-self in an unfamiliar territory, which is neither friendly nor welcoming.

I was transported over to 'A' wing, a large house block that accommodated a few hundred inmates. I was escorted to my cell and closed in for the night and many after that.

Apart from work parties, meal times, gym and association that is where you would remain. Security was tight and governed by stringent ruling. There was no messing about and governor's report meant a trip down to 'chokey', where the walls were as black as the block wardens' hearts.

I managed to get a job in the kitchen, which is a cushy number, and gets you away from the mainframe of prison life. I enjoyed the perks, like eating as much of the slop that is available and peeling as many potatoes as I could before the next meal was due.

I can't honestly say that I enjoyed my time there, but it certainly lived up to what was promised at one of her majesty's hotels. Men were even made or broken here and cannabis was a keen recreational pursuit, which tempered my disposition – it kept the anger at bay.

Security is tight in most prisons, but when a man is incarcerated, he will go to any length to acquire the things that he has come to be accustomed to. Visits from the family are depended on to keep relationships working, but they are also abused, as are family members.

Drugs are smuggled in during visits and a spouse, girlfriend, sibling, parent, even just a friend, are relied on to bring them to the prison and act as a mule to transport illicit substances that an inmate may require.

There is hardly any thought to the danger or consequences of the individual being caught. I have witnessed and participated in showing my disapproval to my visitor for not bringing me in any drugs.

The process of drug trafficking is quite degrading, as orifices are used to stop the contraband from being detected, never mind other implications, such as rectal pain, bleeding, rectal prolapse and even cancer. The rectum is meant for the passing of waste, but in prison it's used as a safe box, which might account for the interest shown by some degenerates who would violate a man's dignity.

The humiliation doesn't end there for the visitor. Women often use their vagina to carry the parcel into the visiting room and then whomever they are visiting removes it, under the scrutiny of the screws that are not just in the room, but also monitoring closely through CCTV.

The so-called clever ones don't take risks; instead they exploit or intimidate the more naïve to risk themselves and loved ones. These are your standard drug dealers, in it for just the profit, but at no cost to themselves.

I was drug dependant for many years and I never realized the effect that it was having on my family, friends and loved ones. Instead, I would look forward to visits and the nights/days ahead getting high.

My time in Dartmoor was coming to an end, as I was considered for parole. This would depend on my behaviour and attitude before my pending discharge date.

I was excited and went to work as usual in the kitchen. The day previously, I had peeled three dustbins full of spuds and was ahead of my duties. I'd hoped to take it easy in the small TV room, which was used during breaks. On entering the kitchen, I couldn't locate the potatoes that were needed for the day's meals.

As I was expressing my concerns, some lanky, long-haired lout mocked my distress and I impulsively 'nutted' him to the floor. The principle officer came marching down the aisle, shouting out orders and stopped right in front of me. He looked at the guy picking himself off the floor and sent me back to the wing.

I returned to my cell and lay on my bed, thinking over what I had just done. Hindsight is good, but I needed to develop foresight if I was going to prevent these destructive patterns from repeating themselves.

I heard footsteps outside my cell and the door was opened by a screw, who told me that the wing P.O. wanted to see me in his office. This was located on the '2s' and I went downstairs to see him. I knocked the office door and was invited in. He was a large friendly-looking man and he offered me a seat on the opposite side of the desk he sat at.

"Shepard, you are in a precarious place," he remarked. He continued with: "If you are nicked for the assault, you won't be paroled and will have to do extra time." If there was a God, this was one of the times that I needed Him. The P.O. mentioned that I should leave it with him, to discuss with his colleague what the outcome should be. I was then returned to my cell, which had an even colder feel than before.

The answer wasn't as quick as I would have liked it and I was starting to feel remorse and regret for my actions. Eventually, I was called back to the office and was told that, although there would be no nicking, I had lost my job and would spend the remainder of my sentence behind the door. I'm not sure if I had thanked God for that one or the plenty of other times that I would pray, when it suited me.

I spent the rest of my time exercising, reading and writing. I wrote another poem at this time, spurred on by angst towards the people who had let me down and not been there for me at a time when I needed them. I called it 'Laugh at my feelings':

Laugh at my feelings, make me look a fool!

What do I care, for it's nothing that's new?

Taken for granted, with gullible compassion,

What do I care; it seems that's the fashion.

But it all makes me stronger

And determined to be

The one better off and everyone will see:

I'm not a loser, but one of the strongest

After all, he who laughs last

Laughs the loudest and longest!

It was during this time away that I became acquainted with a guy called Cripps. He was a bit of a flash git and told me about his earning a lucrative income outside. I became intrigued and started up a friendship with him, hoping to meet up when we got out.

I did indeed catch up with him and he whisked me off to a restaurant in Bristol and bought me a lavish meal, with champagne. I was impressed and when he took me to a nightclub after and asked me if I was interested in a nice little earner, I was up for it.

We checked into a hotel in Bath, which he paid for and proceeded to spend a large amount of money, over the next couple of days. I had a job and a girlfriend back in Gosport, but this was definitely more exciting and I wanted more.

We burgled wealthy homes around the Avon area and would target isolated houses in the countryside. We enjoyed the proceeds of our hauls and wasted it on high living. I didn't particularly like Cripps - he was too smug, but I didn't let that get in the way of business.

We left a club one night and went to a kebab house, to get something to eat on the way back to our hotel. As we were standing in the queue, two girls dressed up as 'St Trinians' girls' came into the shop. I asked them if they were hungry and got Cripps to order two extra Donna kebabs. They came back to the hotel and we stayed up all night. I was attracted to one girl called Jess and we started dating. I decided to leave Gosport and move up to Bath.

Jess and I moved into a bedsit and I'd leave her alone there while I went out on a job with Cripps. I'd even disappear for the weekend and drive down to Gosport and see my uncle.

Sometime after, Cripps and I were driving around in Sussex, casing properties to break into. We had parked up, as Cripps' motor was a canary yellow Capri and stood out like a sore thumb and it wasn't exactly inconspicuous.

After breaking into a promising-looking house and rooting around looking for valuables, we collected some objects together that appeared to be antiques. I was curious as to how we were going to transport it all to the car that was parked half a mile away. Cripps had disappeared and I assumed that he was elsewhere in the house. All of a sudden, I heard a car pull up outside. I looked through an upstairs window and, to my horror; it was Cripps in the Capri. I hadn't noticed a neighbor who had been in his garden opposite. We loaded up and set off to get rid of the swag.

I didn't see Cripps for a couple of days until he turned up at my uncle's, after ringing me and saying he needed to talk to me. When he turned up, he was as white as a ghost and I could see that something was troubling him. It turned out that the neighbor had become suspicious and had talked to the police, who then wanted to interview Cripps. My gut feeling told me that he wouldn't stand up to it and that he would crumble and so I told him not to do anything until I had thought about it.

I knew that I was in breach of my parole and that this was a serious matter if it went to court. I decided to get away and entertained the notion of joining the foreign legion, without a thought for my girlfriend. I arranged to meet with Cripps and told him to give me £500 up front and that I planned on catching a ferry to France and he was not to talk to the police until after I had got through the customs. He was just to tell the old bill that I had used the car and leave it to me to answer their questions if and when I returned.

He got his old man involved and he tried to mug me off with £50, but I told him that his son had got us caught and, if he wanted him to take the flack, and then feel free. I got the £500 and said goodbye to my girlfriend, Jess, and went back to Gosport to say some goodbyes there too. I'd got reacquainted with my childhood sweetheart, Alison, and took her out the day before I was to set off. I gave her a mini that I had purchased and spent the majority of the money that I had earned on her. It was time to go and I caught the ferry from Portsmouth to Cherbourg. I had a mixture of feelings and I didn't know what to expect, but I was determined not to go back to jail. When I arrived in France, I had problems at passport control because I only had a one-way ticket and I was told that I had insufficient funds to travel down to Paris, Marseilles, or Lyons to enlist. I argued with an immigration officer and attempted to walk straight through, but an armed gendarme standing nearby insisted that I got back on the boat.

On my return to England, I tried to raise additional funds by stealing luggage and robbing a shop office on the ship. I discarded all that was of no use to me overboard. I hadn't taken any notice of the contents in a leather case, because it had only held papers and some kind if register.

Just before disembarkation, there was a tannoy loudspeaker announcement to alert passengers to present passports. I didn't know this was a ruse to apprehend me. I had been clocked boarding the ship by someone who had been aware of a police check on persons leaving via airports and on ferries.

Sussex police came on board to escort me back to their local nick, but not before asking me if I'd seen anything of the ship's log. I thought of the paperwork that I'd emptied into the English Channel and I suddenly felt embarrassed as well as annoyed for my plans being skippered. At this stage, I hadn't fully realized the implication of my arrest.

I later found out that Cripps had bottled it and he had 'bubbled me up' for everything, following a raid at his mum's house and a lot of stolen goods being found. He lied about it being mine; he also told the police that it came from jobs that I had done and that he had nothing to do with it. He made out that he had been an unwilling participant and had been in fear of me.

I, on the other hand, kept my part of the deal that we had agreed on and said that I had used his car and done the job in the trainers that were found in his boot, two sizes too small for me. The old bill must have guessed that I was lying, especially when the shoes didn't fit and he had a lot of previous for it.

I was charged and I was sent to Lewes Crown Court for sentencing. I was remanded in HMP Lewes.

I asked Cripps if he could bring Alison up to see me and he seemed eager to please. He'd tried to keep up the pretence of not doing me a wrong and of only trying to help me. A visit was booked.

On the day of my visit, I exercised and washed in my cell. I had another cell, on the '4s', with a window that looked right over the perimeter wall and into a car park situated on the other side of the road of the prison. It was just coming up to visiting time and as I looked out of the window, I recognized a car pulling up, with a man driving and a woman in the passenger seat. The motor came to a still and I observed the two occupants turn to embrace each other and kiss. I was fuming; it was that bloody Capri again and my mate was kissing my girlfriend. Both these people had lied and cheated on me. Being betrayed by a first love and a close acquaintance was too much. I kept my anger down whilst on the visit, until Cripps passed me the ounce of soap bar that he'd brought up. I then told them to both f--k --f and went back to my cell and got stoned.

I was sentenced to 18 months and I served the rest of my time in HMP Camphill, on the Isle of Wight.

This proved to be a testing time for me and it was a very hostile and intimidating environment. It was more like the *'killing fields'*, but with convicts fighting over power, possession and position and I was stuck in the middle of it. The London villains and wannabe gangsters fought to make a name for them-selves. Then there were the bullies, who weren't liked by either side.

I wasn't particularly the biggest of guys in the gym; there were a lot of big blokes that were banging out some heavy weights. One of these cons was called Rawlinson and he was a giant. I looked up to him and thought it would be cool to lift what he could and look like he did, until one day when he mugged me right off. I was checking him out and he said something like, "Don't watch me w-----, go and do your own thing." Not even thinking, I replied, "There's only one w----- here mate and it isn't me!" That went down like the Titanic and I thought there may be trouble ahead. I was right because he accosted me in the changing rooms, grabbing me and throwing me to the floor. He offered me out, but I was having none of it. I got dressed and hurried back to my wing, but was confronted by a couple of huge black men.

"You got to do him blood!" they taunted me with their yardie slang.

I thought, S*od that, look at the size of you two, why don't you two do him?'* I ignored them and went about my own business.

The next time I was at the gym, I'd been getting on with my own thing and was lying down doing some reps of bench press. Without any warning, I suddenly got sucker punched in the left side of my mouth, causing it to split. I looked up and saw Rawlinson looming over me, getting ready to take another shot, while I was helpless with the Olympic bar on my chest. There must have been someone watching over me because he was disturbed by the PTI coming back. I have to admit, fear had filled me with adrenaline and I sucked in my bleeding lip and banged out a few extra reps.

I went back to my wing, ignoring more taunts of others who had themselves been victims of Rawlinson's bullying tactics. No one argued with him and he had a free reign on the adjacent wing to mine, including taxing inmates of their canteen and other valuables.

I was looking at another year in this s—t hole and didn't fancy taking it from him or anyone else, but wasn't sure of what I was going to do about it. I'd never relied on anybody else and my days of being pushed around were over.

Whilst in the prison library, a book had caught my attention and it was one of those oriental mystical types, which define people by symbolic numbers and letters in a person's name - 'numerology'. According to this book, by adding up my date of birth and numbers that are allocated to letters in my name, my primary number was '9'. The book stated that the characteristics of this number are courage, determination and will. I liked the sound of that and was encouraged by it. I sat up that night, repeating that I had these traits, over and over again. I woke up the following day, feeling like Sugar Ray Leonard before a title fight. I was ready for my next gym session that morning and walked on air to the sports hall. As I got changed into vest and shorts, I looked around for my fearsome opponent and he was nowhere to be seen. I bent down to do up my plimsolls and bang, I felt pain in my nose. Looking up, I saw the northern lout grinning as I wiped blood from my face. I threw a left, followed by two right jabs and caught him unexpectedly. I saw surprise in his eyes and continued to jab him again and again. Other inmates had gathered in a circle around us and were jeering me on. Rawlinson lunged at me and grabbed me in a bear hug, lifting me off the ground and throwing me aside like a ragdoll. As I was still lying on the floor, he lifted a full metal dustbin above his head and threw it at me. I managed to avoid it and jumped back to my feet. I started throwing another combination at him, hitting him squarely on the nose and he flinched, saying, "Enough!" I duly obliged and made the mistake of turning away from him. He caught me in the mouth with a massive right, cracking a front tooth. That was it; I lunged at him, throwing everything I had at him. I caught him with a left hook and sent him over a washbasin, where I pummeled him until the fight was broken up by a PTI, insisting: "Alright, nipper, he's had enough." We were taken away to the gym office and the screw asked us both to make up, following which I obliged.

The following day, I was jogging around the football pitch at the sports hall and I heard a shout behind me. Turning around, I saw Rawlinson coming towards me with a massive black geezer and for a moment my ass went.

"Did you say that you can do me?" Rawlinson asked. I noticed the two black eyes and this giant didn't seem so opposing anymore and I replied, "No, but if you want some, we can go again!"

Things changed after that and I was left to my own devices. I served a year on the island, up until I was given home leave and didn't return. My days of taking s—t were over and from now on I decided that I was going to call the shots.

CHAPTER TEN

Starting a Family

In 1985, I spent four weeks on the run from prison and then got picked up and returned to my local nick in Winchester. I lost 28 days' remission, but got them back shortly after because of overcrowding in the jails. I was given an early release, what a result!

I went back to Gosport and dossed about, stealing, drinking and sleeping with girls that I met in the bars. I still used the Green Dragon and it was here that I met a friend of mine called Elaine. She was a single mother of three and offered to put me up at hers, on her sofa. She lived in the maisonettes that I had lived in with my father, before leaving home. My father, his wife and family had since moved into a three-bed roomed house not far away.

Elaine was a heavy drinker too and we would argue a lot, but she would let me get away with murder. I saw her as a big sister, as she was only a couple of years older than me. I took her oldest son, James, under my wing and told him to stay on the straight and narrow and get a job. I didn't want him to follow in my footsteps and become a crook.

Ellie was seeing a Jock called Duncan, from down the pub. He was a hard b-----d and he could drink. We used to go drinking together and I knew that he had my back. During one daytime drinking session down in the town, we had come to the end of our money, but hadn't had enough beer. I decided to pop into Top Man and help myself to a nice suit. Duncan thought that he might try and grab one too, but as we were walking out of the shop, a couple of staff, including the shop manager, grabbed hold of him. They wrestled in the shop doorway and the manager asked him for the suit back. Duncan wasn't willing to oblige and, anticipating him kicking off, I leaned in to him and whispered to him, "Let it go and I'll share the sale of mine." He wasn't having any of it; whether it was his pride or the drink in him, he threatened to knock the staff out. Just then the police pulled up at the kerb. I told Duncan that I had to go and, as I was walking off, a copper on a motorbike pulled up alongside me and asked me where I thought I was going. I told him that I was going down the station to wait and carried on walking. Momentarily confused, the cop let me go and I went off and sold the suit that I had concealed in my leather jacket. When I got home a little later, I asked Ellie if she'd heard from Duncan and she hadn't. So I agreed to go with her down the station after I'd got ready to go out that night.

Bathed, shaved and changed, I got on a bus with Ellie to the town. We planned on going down to the nick and then on for a drink. I was all dressed up and looking forward to a night out with the £50 that I'd got for the suit, when I heard Ellie scream. I turned to see her looking out of the window on the other side of the bus. There was someone holding an elderly guy over the bonnet of a car and punching him repeatedly. What incensed me more was the fact that it was a busy road with so-called upright citizens walking straight past, oblivious to the old boy's distress. I shouted out of a small sliding window "Leave him alone!" and, to my amazement, this nut job ran to the front of the bus trying to punch the driver through his open window. The driver panicked and tried to pull away, but I moved to the exit and told him to stop the bus. I got off and walked around the bus and asked the guy what his problem was and he replied, "Do you want some too?"

I thought '*sod this*' and threw a combination at the dude and as he went down he grabbed hold of my shirt, ripping all the buttons off. I lost it and kicked him in the head, only stopping when I looked up and saw the look on Ellie's face. I grabbed the guy off the floor and, lifting him up to his feet, I told him to apologize. He said, "Sorry," and I replied, "Not to me, idiot!" and pushed him towards the elderly guy who was now standing beside the car. Other people seemed interested now and so I got back on the bus. As I got on, the driver mentioned something about the assailant being lucky that he was on probation and I just told him to drive. I walked to the back of the bus and sat down. An old lady, who was sitting opposite and had witnessed the whole thing, got up and came over and kissed me on the cheek. She told me that it had been very noble and I just turned and smiled at Ellie, who seemed in a much calmer state.

Little did I know, but the elderly gent was a local dignitary and had asked the local paper to print a 'thank you' to the Good Samaritan that had stopped and helped him. That article actually prevented me from receiving a lengthy prison sentence a little later on. I was on remand for a list of offences and had been brought up to Portsmouth Crown Court for sentencing. The prosecution had put up a good case and I was looking at a bit of bird. Suddenly, my barrister got up and mentioned that, although the judge had heard some derogatory things about me, there were some mitigating factors that he'd like the judge to take into consideration. This was the first I'd heard of the newspaper article and the judge seemed intrigued. After my barrister had presented all my case, the judge asked me to stand. He told me that my record was not a good one and that he had no other choice but to give me a lengthy prison sentence. However, he was giving me credit for my bravery and that it merited him giving me a suspended sentence with a community service order. I was free to go.

Ellie put me up again and things were much the same, except that I had started working. I got a job with a local building firm, after convincing them that I was a bricklayer. I'd done a City & Guilds whilst in prison, but never completed the course or the exam because of time down the 'block'. I needed transport to get about and bought a car. I still hadn't passed my driving test and so was an unlicensed and uninsured driver. (I'd been driving illegally for a few years by now.) It was an old Escort and I bought it because it looked good, but I knew nothing of cars and it was just an old banger, which was soon off the road.

On my way to the pub one afternoon I bumped into Ellie, who was walking with a friend of hers called Claire. We got talking and I soon learnt that she lived up the posh end of The Spinney and was the daughter of one of the nicer neighbors that we hadn't talked to whilst growing up. I remembered her vaguely and found it interesting how we had lived so close to each other for so long, but knew nothing of each other. She said that she had heard things about me and I thought: 'That's the end of that then.' But there was a spark and we started seeing each other.

We moved in together and rented a room from the neighbor of a friend. Claire was a straight girl and I think I might have tried to keep up the pretence of being a nice lad, but my drinking always betrayed me and I would end up doing things I would regret. Like the time I came back from the pub drunk and did a smash and grab on a local Co-op, grabbing money from the till and as many cigarettes as I could carry.

Claire put up with a lot, but the landlord wouldn't take any nonsense and we had to move out.

Claire fell pregnant and I wasn't prepared for adulthood, never mind parenting. I was neither mature or responsible enough and still liked to mess around through the drink and the drugs. More often than not, I would find myself in someone else's bed after a drunken one-night stand and the feelings that I was left with were more than condemning.

Claire came to her senses and jogged me on, much to my disappointment. I had been looking forward to being a father, but for all the wrong reasons. I thought that I could actually make a better parent than my own, with all the issues that I had.

My daughter, Amber, was born and she was a beautiful, dark-haired girl, with the softest of brown eyes. I immediately fell in love with this wonderful little being, but I didn't really know what to do about it. I worked hard on building sites as a hod-carrier and made sure that she had all the baby equipment that was needed. I handed over a tax rebate that I had received to Claire and visited Amber as much I could.

Around the same time, I found lodgings with a single mother called 'Tisha', who lived on a local estate. She was young and impressionable and thought that I might be a good catch. I shared her bed but not her intentions, and instead solicited myself for her affection. I was approached one day by her friend, who mentioned to me that Tisha hoped to entrap me by falling pregnant. I wasn't impressed with the suggestion and found it unbelievable. The friend had also told me that she was not taking the contraceptive pill that she was prescribed. I rushed back to the flat and, on searching, found full packets of the pill down the side of the stereo. She did indeed fall pregnant, but I wasn't going to be forced into committing to a loveless relationship and left without taking any responsibility.

I continued to sleep around and wasn't concerned about anyone else's feelings except my own.

In 1988, I met the woman who would become the mother of my two beautiful girls – Maxine and Katie.

One night I went to a 21st birthday of a friend of mine, named Steve. As Steve and I entered the club that the party was held in, I surveyed the dance floor to see who was there. I saw two girls dancing together and, although one of them was familiar, I didn't recognize the other one. Steve went to the bar to buy the drinks and I approached the two dancers. I audaciously grabbed hold of a short blond-haired girl and swung her around with a tango move. I then put her down and walked away from them, but heard the one that I had just released say, "That's my kind of man."

I must admit, it fuelled my ego and it is quite possible that is why I took it further. The two girls invited us to another club that they were going to, but I wasn't dressed for it and so Steve declined but leant me his trousers. I must have looked a doughnut, because his waistband was several sizes larger than mine. But, then again, he had to wear my jeans home, which would probably have caused him more embarrassment. I dropped Ness off that night and never slept with her, because I had learned that she was living with someone and had a daughter, called Tasha. It didn't stop me though, as she had given me her number and we arranged to see each other again.

I started to see her while her partner was at work. She had mentioned that she didn't love him and that she had lost respect for him, since he had left her while she was pregnant. But the truth is I didn't care about what I did or who I hurt. I did tell her that I didn't do 'second best' and that I wasn't going to be the other man. She decided to leave him and we shacked up at a friend of hers for a little while, until her ex said that she and Tasha could move back into the house, as long as I didn't. She took him up on his offer, but moved me in too. We never told him and he would come round every Sunday to pick up his little girl. I would be sitting in the lounge next to the front door and I could hear him telling her to leave me and he would come back.

One Sunday, I had had enough and so he wouldn't know that I was there, I left through the back door. I came round to the front and said, "Alright love?" He jumped in his car and sped off. I must admit, I often wondered if the right guy drove off.

It was our first Christmas together and Ness invited Claire and Amber over for dinner. I thought it was kind of her, but it still didn't stop me from feeling awkward being with them both together.

Not long after, Claire started dating again and had been told by a fortune-teller that she would meet and marry someone in the army. Shortly after, a soldier came along and she told me that she didn't want any more maintenance as she was getting married and that he'd be Amber's daddy.

At first I disagreed and said no one was taking my place as her father and was adamant that it wouldn't happen. A friend of mine, named Tim, invited me to his son's birthday and his wife said, "Look, Amber, it's your daddy."

To my horror, my beautiful little girl replied, "No, he's my other daddy." Wrong that it may have been, feeling a little crushed, I walked away and let someone else become a dad to my daughter. My decision was aided by the fact that Ness had given birth to my first daughter, Maxine, and she had reminded me that my family was now here with her and the two girls. This was ironic because Tasha never stayed with us and at this time my youngest had not yet been born.

I'd also fathered another daughter called Naomi, but was never present to be a dad to her. I attempted to be a dad to Tasha and Maxine, but my heart wasn't really in fatherhood and I was seldom ever there.

It was about this time that I was approached by a couple of dealers, to sell some dope and some speed. I had often sat in the 'Green Dragon', admiring a certain clique there. They appeared to be a part of the 'in crowd', with an entourage that followed them. They always had money, nice cars and fast women and whatever they were up to, they never seemed to get caught. I was instantly attracted to their way of life.

I was approached by a couple of these men, who wanted me to take some drugs off them, on credit. I never thought twice about repercussions or consequences and jumped right in.

CHAPTER ELEVEN

Hell Has Begun

When you sell drugs, everyone wants to be your friend and girls are drawn to you because of what you have, rather than who you are. I would spend the days running around 'wheeling & dealing' and nights down the pub. I never got to see my daughters grow up and was constantly getting nicked, with the front door going through on countless busts. I would be carted away to the local nick for questioning and, if the old bill were fortunate enough to get anything on me, then I would be facing time in the jail at Winchester.

I actually thought that I was clever when the police couldn't make charges stick but, instead of taking caution or learning from my mistakes, I treated it as a game and called it 'them and us'.

I was now distant from any relatives, including my dad and step-brothers and sisters. This was the result of assaulting both my dad and my step-mother, in retaliation for their many assaults on me.

One evening, I had come in from work after a hard day's graft and an upset with my old friend Chris, who had threatened Claire while she was pregnant. I was sitting at the kitchen table at my father's house, as he had put me up after a short stint in prison. Nikki was running away at the mouth about my being late and I thought this was comical because, not only was I about 22 years old, but it was 6 o'clock in the evening. So, I told her to 'do one' and she totally lost it, jumped up then ran over to me and slapped me round the face. I wasn't having it, woman or not, and slapped her back. My dad then came running into the dining room and he was a big bloke. I said, "Enough! I'm leaving!" and as I walked out of the lounge to enter the hall by the front door, she wacked me with the phone and I slapped her harder. She fell backwards and started to call the police as I walked out the front door. I heard a shout behind me and turned to see my dad thundering towards me. In a moment, I was seeing all the hidings that he had given me as a boy and I said, "Don't, Dad, I'm not a kid any longer." He ignored my warning and charged me. I threw a left so fast that neither of us saw it coming and when it connected, it lifted all 17 stone of this big man off his feet and launched him onto the garden path next door. I walked out of his gate and slammed it behind me. I made for the bus stop just round the corner from where my dad lived and fell to the floor, sobbing my heart out. Pedestrians walked by, looking at me, but I really didn't care how I might have looked, I was gutted for hitting my dad. Shortly afterwards, an ambulance appeared and turned into my dad's road. Moments later it was back and it stopped at a junction, just long enough for me to open the door and see my dad getting up from the stretcher, growling at me. I closed the door again and left the scene as he was taken away.

Sometime after I called my dad to apologize, but he wasn't having any of it and said that they had pressed charges. It later went on to court and my stepmother stood in the dock and lied, with the intention of getting me convicted, but she wasn't consistent with her statement. The sad thing was that my dad lied too and I understood that he felt compelled because of his love for this woman, but it reflected a lack of love for me. I was acquitted on the grounds of self-defense, but this was not accepted by her and there was a heavy strain on the relationship with my father from then on.

However, I received a call from Claire, stating that Nikki had taken some fancy fellow round to hers and she was concerned that Nikki was having an affair. I called my dad's house and he answered the phone. I asked if she was there and could he put her on the phone. I then told her to stay away from Claire's as she had nothing to do with her. I also told her that if she carried on with any affair, that I would tell my dad. She made her own choice and my father found himself in another wrecked marriage. This broke him and the pressure of looking after five kids on his own contributed to his bad health.

I never really had a father and son relationship with him, but we shared a brief time in that place before I got sent back to prison in 1990 for reckless driving. I visited him while he was alone and told him what I had been up to and he never judged me, and instead offered to help. I wasn't able to receive this at the time and kept my visits minimal.

I'd just got jailed for two years for the driving offence, after writing a police car off in a chase, when I'd failed to stop. Nessa was pregnant again with Katie and I was in Winchester, working down in the kitchen as the prison butcher. One of the kitchen orderlies came into my work area and mentioned that a couple of screws upstairs were talking about me. Being the bolshie git that I was, I shot through the kitchen, vaulted over the hot-plate and raced upstairs to the wing office. A couple of prison officers stopped talking as I walked in, uninvited.

"What's going on then?" I asked.

They both looked at each other and urged the other to tell me something. I stood there bemused for a moment and then I was asked to follow the senior up onto the 'two's' to the chapel. He unlocked the gate and we walked through to the back, where the office was situated. The officer said to the assistant chaplain, "You tell him." I was about to let them have it, when I was pointed to a phone and asked to ring my partner. Now this is normally a perk that is left to the discretion of the chaplain and he normally makes the call. Without any hesitation, I rang my girlfriend up and asked what was going on. Everything seemed to stand still and attention was focused on me and my reaction.

"Your dad's dead," was all I heard, except that she was coming up that afternoon. I turned and asked the officer to take me back down to D1 landing and didn't say another thing.

On the day of my father's funeral I was escorted to Portsmouth crematorium by two prison officers. I remained handcuffed all through the service, much to the disapproval of other family members. They were angry at me for bringing dishonor to my father's name and made it known vocally.

On being transported back to the prison, I returned to my cell and didn't grieve openly. Several days later I was called up in front of the governor and told that I was to attend a court hearing over maintenance for Naomi – the daughter that I had fathered with Tisha. I was also told that, as there was a shortage of staff, I couldn't be escorted and would be given a day's home leave. I felt infuriated, as it seemed that I hadn't been allowed to show respect to my dead father, but was permitted to be let out for a civil matter. I went to court and then returned to the jail. The next day, I put in a request to see the governor and put it to him that I would like to grieve my father properly. I stated that I had been allowed to be released to court without escort and felt that if I wasn't regarded as a security risk for one matter, that it should be so for the other. I was granted a day's home leave and spent some time with friends, getting drunk and high. I managed to get back and through reception without any qualms.

That happened to be the only time that I received a D Cat status and enjoyed the benefits of being in an open prison. I was transferred to HMP Ford and stayed there for a month, before being transferred again to IRC Haslar. I was able to have town visits at the weekend and was also let out for the birth of my youngest daughter, Katie.

Previous to her birth, I had wangled time out during the Christmas of '91. Normally, prisons have a shut down period from mid December until early January. I had been given notice of a 4-day compassionate leave, on the arrival of our child. On a Christmas Eve morning, I had rung Nessa and we had talked about her having labour pains. I insisted that she call the midwife, who in turn called the prison. That evening, as I was just settling down for Christmas locked up behind bars, a screw called 'Blighty' came down to our unit and announced:

"Come on, Shep; wish your mates Happy Christmas."

I couldn't believe it, I was being released and allowed home to see my family. I got dressed quickly and headed for reception, to change into my civilian clothes. A taxi was called and I was taken home to the girls.

I spent the evening at home and woke up the next day to watch the kids open their presents. We then all went down to Nessa's mums and I was given a glass of punch. I had to report back to the prison because of conditions on my warrant. I got through to a reception officer, who didn't sound that happy, especially when he was told that it might be a false alarm. Unfortunately, the governor was stood right beside him and ordered me to return – immediately. I felt that I should oblige, as I didn't want anything to affect my attendance at the actual arrival. On return, I was greeted by a very stern looking governor, who insisted in a shrill voice that I get back to my unit. Things did die down though and on the 27th January the following year, my fourth daughter was born. I was actually allowed to attend the hospital and complete the 4-day compassionate leave.

Anyone in the right frame of mind would have been content to have been given a family of their own. But drink and drugs were now being consumed much more heavily and seriously affected my judgement.

I was constantly looking for a way to earn cash because of my reckless lifestyle and was consumed with all manner of rogue behaviour. Addiction, offending and infidelity were at the top of the list and I masked it all with bravado. I made excuse after excuse for my behaviour and attitude, blaming others and justifying the cause of it all. I was in serious denial and wouldn't listen or take anyone's advice – what was I afraid of?

Drugs are a good way of escaping or attempting to bury something that you do not like or want and my emotions were difficult and very unpleasant.

I progressed to harder drugs like cocaine, after coming out of prison and being visited by an old cellmate. It was at this time that I met a lovable rogue called Colin, who became more of a friend than associate. We shared the same interests of coke, beer, pubs and pool (in that order). It was to be our downfall and his demise.

I had been given a Sierra Sapphire to sell or buy and given time to make the payment of £4,500. I approached a Ford dealer and was told that they would give me the purchase price, which meant I might make a profit by selling it privately.

I'd asked around but had no joy, until I approached my friend Colin. He suggested that we take it to some friends of his who might be interested. We started at a pub in Fareham called 'The Highlands' and were soon enjoying the company of a bunch of local lads. Colin had put us up in a few games of 'doubles', which we won and were bought drinks for.

During the course of the evening, we ended up in a boozer on the outskirts of Fareham and the rest of the memory remains uncertain. I awoke from a 4-day coma, with a policeman at the end of my bed and was accused of 'causing death by dangerous driving' to my friend Colin.

His partner had been deeply distressed and had suggested that I was to blame and this was reinforced by others saying that I had switched places in the car immediately after the accident. I was too traumatized to be incensed at the outrageous allegation. Seriously - could I possibly have dragged my mate, from one seat to the other, before collapsing into a coma?

I remained in hospital for a couple of weeks as I was being treated for broken bones in my back and my left arm. My ribcage concaved around my heart, which prevented it from being set back in place. The hospital administered morphine to me, which dulled both the physical and mental pain. This was later to have an adverse effect on me, as I was constantly seeking the numbness of any pain that I may have been carrying.

The case went to trial and I was told that I was facing up to 8 years in prison. I was confused, afraid and alone, but as much as I felt regret and remorse for my friend's death – it was still a tragic accident. The court finally reached a decision on a lesser charge. An independent examiner presented his report, with calculations in my defense, and no other evidence was given contrary to his findings. Yet I'll never forget that year, as 1994 was the year that all hell had begun. I might have been acquitted by the court, but I was still considered guilty by others.

I flew to southern Spain with some friends to get away and stayed at an apartment with a group of people who were experimenting with a new drug. I stayed out there for just over a week, but I returned with something that should never have been allowed access into mine or my children's lives – heroin.

On my return, I continued to smoke cannabis and use speed, but now I had an additional dependency that demanded first place and constant gratification. When I first put the aluminium foil tube in my mouth and inhaled the smoke off the sheet, I did not know or realize that I was handing my soul over to the devil and eating his candy.

CHAPTER TWELVE

Looking For a Solution

The devil knows our torment because he is the one who instigates it, then sits back and mocks as you hand over your life, your respect and your dignity for the price of a 'bag'. He has been using such tactics since way back in the beginning of the first century. And his mask is deception and his lies are the keys to a man's soul. His goal is to impart fear, guilt and shame, which will then lead to desolation, degradation and finally, despair.

On reflection, I can't help but think about all the time that I spent in solitary confinement as a prisoner. I can now see that I was never really free. I was held captive in a place that is deep in a man's soul. The soul is the combination of the mind, will and emotions. It's the place where our own identity is created and determines

91

how we perceive ourselves in the world around us.

I never believed or understood that there was any other place that I could ever be. I wasn't at liberty to enjoy the freedom that is available, as I believed that I was born bad and that was just the way that it had to be. I fed this lie with my own vain imaginations and the deception that often accompanied it.

King Solomon of the Bible wrote in the book of Proverbs many wise sayings. But the one that fully expresses this false preconception of mine is:

"*For as he thinks in his heart, so is he [in behaviour—one who manipulates].*" *(Proverbs 23:7 – Amplified Bible)*

I became dependent on heroin and it fully took over my life. I never imagined the depths that it would take me to, or what I would be prepared to give up for it. I had, up till then, still held certain values and injecting into my veins had been a big 'no…no.' I once caught a friend with a needle in his arm and rebuked him, showing nothing but contempt and disdain. I had also turned heroin down many times before in prison and looked down on the users, rather than be sympathetic towards them.

Yet all that was forgotten as the addiction increased and placed more demands on me to feed it.

The first time I injected was whilst bailed to a hostel in Gloucester. I had been charged with intent to supply cannabis, speed and LSD. I had been wronged by a friend who had got close to me. He had been welcomed into my home and sat with my family – he had been trusted.

I had been involved with some drug dealers and some animosity and hostility had developed towards me and other associates. A young friend of mine had been threatened and there was supposed to be a price on him getting done over. A local thug, who was supposed to be a bit tasty, had agreed to sort my mate out and I said that I would take care of it. So I visited the thug and made it clear that if he or anyone else touched my friend, that he would be the one who would be getting it.

The thing was, my mate who had been threatened, had owed me some money and had taken a 'bar' on 'tick' off of a dealer, who had become incensed. The fact that I had warned off his 'heavy' made him furious and he hatched a plan to set me up. He then approached the friend that had got close to me and asked him to supply a number of microdots (LSD). They arranged to meet in one of the local pubs and do the transaction. My old friend clearly wasn't thinking straight and walked in carrying them and was met by old bill.

Sometime after, he was bailed and released and came to my house. The following morning at the crack of dawn, my front door was kicked in and my house was full of armed police. My little girls cried as their daddy was taken away to the station and I was remanded to Winchester nick.

Whilst on remand, the so-called friend that had set me up came to the prison to visit me and admitted that he had been coerced by the police to implicate me. He made a statement to my solicitor at the time and a court date was set. He then went on the run and when he was apprehended by the police, told them that I had forced him at gunpoint to make a statement. As ridiculous as it sounded, the police went along with it and charged both my solicitor and me with perverting the course of justice. The copper in the case, named Norcross, did his best to make it stick and also charged my brief with money laundering.

During the trial it came out that the prosecution witness had indeed been offered an inducement and that the officer concerned had made allegations contrary to my solicitor's integrity.

I was released from court and didn't have to return to the hostel. I did however spend up to sixteen months in prison on remand. I was shipped from nick to nick because of the controversy over the trial and spent many months away from my family. I did pen a limerick whilst sitting in the dock waiting for the verdict and staring at the back of Norcross's bald head. He was known by his colleagues as *'Iron-man'* and in particular, *'Snorks'*. So I wrote:

There was a copper called 'Snorks',

Who brought defendants to court?

With wild allegations,

And lies down the station,

Not forgetting the informants he bought.

I showed it to my barrister, who in turn shared it with the bench, as well as other officers - of whom one had mentioned that it would be put up on the notice board of the canteen at the station, much to the disapproval of their unimpressed colleague.

This was the first of several serious court cases that went to trial. I don't mind admitting that, down in the cells underneath the crown courts, I prayed to God for divine intervention and mercy.

Like the time when the police once again encroached upon my liberty, using tactics that would be considered in the USA as entrapment.

I was introduced, through an associate, to someone who wanted to invest a large amount of money - £30,000. Of course I didn't hear any alarm bells because, not only was the introduction made through a trusted associate, but also because the cash register was ringing too loud in my ears, 'ker-ching.'

The guy with the money was introduced to every villain in town and the race was on to see which one of us would get the money first. This guy would buy anything and everything; you could have taken a video out of a skip round to him and he would have given you a good price. Unfortunately, I wasn't the only one who had been duped by his guise, as every addict in Gosport was knocking on his door to fence their 'goods'.

It didn't take long for the front doors to go in and all of us to be rounded up by the old bill at the local nicks. The cells were full and around thirty of us were up before the magistrates on a range of charges from theft to burglary. I was charged with conspiracy to supply class A. I have to admit, my ass went a little when my barrister said I was looking at 12-18 years. They had me on camera giving it Charlie big potato, hoping to impress this goon into handing me over the cash. When my barrister said that it wasn't looking good, as I had been recorded telling a witness that I would supply him with a kilo of heroin, I had to confess. I told him that I was ashamed of my drug habit and was trying to impress. I also mentioned that I didn't have any heroin to give him and that I was hoping that he would hand over the full amount, in order to fleece him. My barrister thought that I should be concerned about this, but that wasn't what I was being charged with. Back in the cells under the crown court, I said a little prayer out loud:

"Heavenly Father, I come to you and ask that you would forgive me and grant me mercy. I can't ask that you get me off because I am guilty of a crime, but if you would just let me have another chance, I promise that I will change!"

I suddenly became suspicious of the one that had made the introduction to me and asked my barrister to ask the court if he was an informant. Consequently, the case was adjourned and when it was in session again, the prosecution stated that:

'The Chief Constable refuses to deny or confirm the identity of an informant and for this reason the Crown does not wish to proceed with this case.'

Repeatedly, I was arrested after false evidence had been gathered, construed and contrived in a derogatory fashion, to implicate me and to coerce others into reaching a prejudiced decision.

I use to enjoy a game of cat and mouse with the police, but this was getting serious. They had targeted me and it had become obvious that they would use any means. People that I knew and had at one time mixed with were rolling over and having their bellies tickled for immunity and inducements. I was experiencing betrayal and treachery all round and did not know whom I could trust.

On top of all this, whilst I was in prison, I heard that Vanessa was seeing my old friend, Chris. I rang a friend called Simon to find out if it was true and his reply was, "You want the truth – she was gagging for it and couldn't get enough". It felt like I had been shot and I returned to my cell, dejected and full of hurt and pain. I thought about killing him, but I realized it had taken two of them to come together and I wasn't prepared to kill my baby's mother. I went back to her on my release, but that was more out of ego than my duty to protect my kids.

If I could have just walked away, I would have, but it was difficult because both Vanessa and I had serious drug problems that don't just disappear overnight. She had already been arrested and threatened with prison and I couldn't risk the girls being without their mum. I was unable to work because of my drug dependency and benefits don't pay enough to even cover all the bills and food. I continued offending to fund both our habits, making the excuse that it was to give my girls a better life (what a load of b-------).

I was desperate to stand by my two youngest daughters; I had already lost two of them and wasn't prepared to lose any more. I was constantly reminded of how my mum had walked out and how I had been left feeling rejected and separated from the one who should love you.

I promised my girls, Max and Kate, that I would never give up trying to beat my addictions until they were defeated – whatever it took.

We lived near a church hall, which is named Jacob's Well. I had heard of it year's earlier but had just made fun of it at the time and yet I suddenly felt drawn to attend a service. I missed attending the prison chapel and I believed that God had spoken to me there. The pastor's name was Rose; she was a lovely, kind figure and there was something 'mumsy' that I liked about her.

Jacob's Well is a Pentecostal church, which means that the Holy Spirit is visible through utterances and prophetic words of God.

During one service, Pastor Rose turned around and exclaimed that new leaders would come from the drug addicts and drunks, while looking straight at me. I found this quite eerie and uncomfortable at first, as the only other experience I'd had of what appeared to be a prediction of sorts, was from psychics, which I understand to be evil. But these people welcomed me, just as I was, and they supported and encouraged me to want to make a difference.

I was still using drugs and would mix the uppers (stimulants) with the downers (depressants). I took heroin to combat the physical withdrawals and speed to hide the symptoms and the drowsiness of the opiates.

I had got into the worship at church and decided that I wanted to be baptized. A few of the church leadership team and some of the congregation attended a baptism at Stokes Bay and I was invited. I took a leap of faith and walked into the sea. I asked Jesus to come into my life. I asked Him if He would forgive me of my sin. I renounced the devil and asked Jesus to take over my life and to lead me. I was then submerged into the sea and then lifted to my feet to walk again. The thing is, when I took off the shirt that I'd been wearing, there had been a bag with an ounce of amphetamine in the top pocket, which I hadn't thrown away. As I put the shirt back on, I heard a voice inside my mind say, "You didn't mean that and you haven't changed." I tried not to think about it, but it was kind of hard to dismiss. I eventually confessed this to the pastoral team at church and we discussed me going to rehab and getting clean.

I didn't act on it straight away and found myself in prison again shortly after. Vanessa and I were not happy in our relationship and were constantly separated. While I was in prison, an old girlfriend came back to Gosport to look me up and was told by my old friend, Chris that I was in Winchester Prison. She wrote to me and then came up on a visit. I was promised a new start and a good job as a recruitment manager for chefs in top hotels. It all sounded good and on my release I went to Essex to make a new start. However, it was short-lived because I could see that she was a manipulative bitch and I had reason not to trust her because she still showed signs of infidelity, as in our previous relationship. Her daughter came on to me too and I succumbed, leaving me feeling no better. During a phone call home, Vanessa asked me if I still loved her and when I hesitated to answer, she urged me to say it. This was overheard by the Essex girl and she suggested that Nessa came and picked me up. A friend of mine loaned her his car and she was on her way.

She picked me up later that night, but we ran out of petrol and ended up parked on the hard shoulder of the motorway. We were eventually towed to a filling station and filled up to return home. Previously, I had rung a rehab in Reading and referred myself. They asked if I could attend an interview. I asked Nessa to take me to the rehab and see if I could get them to take me. I was accepted and, shortly after, I returned to Yeldall Manor to do their program.

Yeldall is a mansion house that has been converted to take up to 20-30 male residents. It is a therapeutic community that relies on the love and discipline needed to follow Christ. Although there's no mention of smoking being prohibited in the process, in fact there is a designated area for the smoking of cigarettes during break, outside of the daily activities of the structured programme. Like most Christian communities, the mornings consist of wake up, breakfast, devotional and then general cleaning. Work duties are then allocated and these take place up to lunch, unless you have appointments elsewhere. Work continues in the afternoon and, after dinner there's generally a Bible class and then a short period of recreation. Residents have the option to read, play pool, watch TV or go for a walk, accompanied by another resident. There are usually stages to complete during the programme and the first is always an induction phase. This is normally meant for the residents to come to terms with where they are, to prepare them for what they have to do on the programme.

During my first month there I had to attend Portsmouth Crown Court again, for another trial. I had been bailed to the rehab and had to sign on at the police station during the week. I was given an overnight stay at home to attend court, which meant that I could indulge in a few drinks and a joint after the hearing.

The next day, on my return to Yeldall, I arrived at the station pick-up point too early and so went into the pub adjacent to the railway. I knocked back a couple of Stellas and appeared quite jovial when my lift turned up to get me. He was one of the counselors there and was not impressed with my turnout. He asked me why I had a drink and I replied that I was thirsty. He then asked me why I had gone into a pub and felt the need to drink alcohol. I looked at him incredulously and remarked flippantly, "Because that's what you do, mate, and besides, I'm not here for the drink but to get off drugs!"

I was driven back to the mansion house and asked to go and have a shower before dinner. The next day I was brought before the director and asked to explain myself all over again. It still didn't register with me that I had transgressed and I wasn't happy when I was put back to the beginning of the programme. But, I didn't make it easy on myself either because I was constantly getting a discipline chit for erroneous behaviour – not shaving, swearing, leaving the light on, and threatening behaviour. These chits are handed out and, if they accumulate, you are required to fulfill a discipline duty while others are taken out swimming and shopping during recreation time. I was constantly left behind to sweep the long, leafy drive leading up to the house. I would also have to go to bed early on Friday and Saturday nights, when others might be enjoying the privilege of a late night. I got round this by waiting till the night-staff member had got his head down and I would sneak upstairs to one of the TV rooms at the top of the house.

Christmas time was looming and I had completed induction. I had requested an overnighter on Christmas Eve to go home to my girls and it had been granted. I worked in the gardens and had just spent the day in one of the fields, cutting a large tree into logs. I was tired and hungry. I finished my meal and asked one of my pals, on the wash up team I was on, if I could be excused. As I sat in the lounge resting and watching a bit of TV, the door opened and one of the residents came in. He stood behind the sofa making snide comments about me not doing my turn. My feelings towards him had been brewing over the past couple of weeks, as I thought him to be a self-righteous twat; and now he was begging for it. I jumped up and chased him into the dining area, stopping only to pick up a chair to put over his nut. As I raised it above my head, I recognized my state of anger and suddenly realized that this wasn't the right thing to do. I was showing typical prison behaviour – the solution to everything was to use manipulation or force. I put the chair down and apologized. I then went to the office and reported my actions to a member of staff. I don't know if I was just trying to be clever or whether I thought that, in doing so, there wouldn't be such harsh consequences. I was wrong. The coming Friday, I was back in front of the Director and sent back to the beginning again. I didn't even give myself time to process my actions or anything. My last thought was that I wasn't going to be there on Christmas Day for my kids. It didn't help that Vanessa had confessed to me about taking heroin. Up to my going away to rehab, she had pushed me to get clean, even offering me an ultimatum – the drug (heroin) or her. We soon found out that if you try to make a choice over that, there's only one loser (you). It seemed pointless in staying to get over it, only to return to it on the completion of my programme, so I left rehab.

It wasn't a complete waste of time because a foundation had been laid for me to build my Biblical faith on.

I continued to spend time in and out of detox units, mainly to try and stay out of prison. I was assessed for other rehabs, but never completed the detox programs. I did a six- week programme once because of a court order and was supposed to stay an extra couple of days after completing the detoxification stage. But I had other ideas; I wanted to go home and gratify my flesh before starting the 3-month 12-step programme. So I left that too and was returned to prison.

I was a prolific needle user and I wanted to give up the use, but not the behaviour that accompanied it. I held onto trophies, such as gold jewellery and the false identity that I had given myself in most of the things that I did. I thought that my life depended on what I had, rather than what I did.

CHAPTER THIRTEEN

Heaven Calls

I was arrested again on a supply charge, but this time it was serious, as it was class A. The sentencing is much steeper and starts at around 4 years (for small amounts). I didn't want to spend my life in prison and knew that heroin was destroying me. I was told about a Christian community in London, which was completely different than any other programme that I had tried. I was keen to make a serious change in my life and decided to give it a go.

Whilst in prison, I had borrowed and read many testimonies of men like myself that had given their life to Jesus and had been transformed by God's power. One of the books that I read was 'The Cross and the Switchblade'. It was the story of a preacher that took the word of God to the gangs in New York. He met a young gang member by the name of Nicky Cruz and it's a story of these young people's redemption. I was touched by how a mighty God should care about a no-good hoodlum and want to show him love and a plan for his life beyond anything that he could imagine. The preacher's name was David Wilkerson and Teen Challenge is the fruit of his ministry in New York. It is a global corporation that works with drug addicts, alcoholics, gang members and others with life controlling habits.

I was told that, if I really wanted to make a go of it, then this was the place that I should start. So I got the number of the London centre and gave them a call.

An interview was arranged for me to visit Wilkerson House in Ilford and I attended a meeting with the manager. He showed me around the house and explained what would be expected of me. The rules are stringent and any breach can result in being asked to leave the programme. There is a no-smoking policy; obviously there are no drink/drugs, illicit or provocative behaviour that can cause harm or injury to oneself or another. This was like an SAS camp for the Christian disciple. I loved the thought of it and thought I'd give it a go.

I had to ring back every day until a bed was available, but it's also a way of showing the person's commitment to want to change.

I got my bed and was given a lift there on the day of my expected arrival. I smoked the last of my fags and even had a few cans before I set off. I was taken to my room and two staff members went through my property, taking anything that wasn't permitted to be kept on my person. I was then taken down into the dining room and a cup of coffee was made for me. As the men finished their work for the day, I was introduced and made to feel welcome by the other residents. The food was good and generous portions were had by those who wanted their fill. After dinner there was a short period of recreation before the classes started. In the classrooms we were taught how to put Bible principles into action. No one was permitted to talk during class, unless spoken to by the staff member. All staff had undertaken, completed and graduated from the programme and so were examples to the rest of us of God's transformation. I looked for their imperfections purposely, although in truth I was probably transferring my own. This didn't stop me taking a dislike to a few members of staff whose authority I found hard to accept. Maybe it was their approach, but I have to say that these men operated out of the Father's love – I just struggled with the acceptance of my father's discipline or should I say abuse?

I wanted to know whether God really existed and was constantly asking Him to show himself in a tangible way. I wasn't prepared for what happened during one of the Sunday services at church.

I had been sitting in my seat during the sermon, looking around at those in attendance - in particular the girls from the women's house. One of them had caught my attention and was trying to ask me how long had I been on the programme already. Suddenly, the pastor who was preaching turned in my direction and his whole countenance changed. His face was shining like the sun and his eyes blazed like fire as he spoke:

"Will you step out of your place of comfort and stop running from me?"

I've got to say that I was shaken up and could not control the violent shaking of my body. When he called me to the front, I was drawn forward and it was like someone else was carrying me. Someone's hands were laid upon me and I started to mumble in a foreign tongue that sounded like gobbled gook to me.

I left that church a different man, but wasn't quite sure what the hell had happened. The following Friday a group of evangelists came to the house and, while the leader was ministering, she asked if anyone needed prayer. At the end of the service I approached her and told her my concerns about what had happened at last week's service, in particular the strange noises coming out of my mouth. She asked me to pray in the spirit and not to be alarmed. I started to pray and that strange language came out of my mouth again but, as I was speaking, she said, "Yes, an over comer!"

Well, I have to say, it was quite an experience and I did like the fact that God called me personally, out of Jesus' mouth. However, if I thought that was all there was to it, I was mistaken. I still continually showed signs of rebellious behaviour, but the final straw was when it was said that I would make a great preacher. I suddenly thought of Teen Challenge like a conveyor belt knocking out replica Christians with no authenticity and I liked the idea of being unique. I was told that I was going to make a great preacher and I thought: 'Hold on, I didn't come here for this!' I suddenly felt a fear of standing on some soapbox preaching: "*Repent, the end is nigh!*" I lost my bottle and made excuses to leave.

The strange thing was that, when I returned to Gosport, people noticed a change in me. I started to tell them about how God had worked in me. I wanted to pull a zip across my mouth, but it kept flowing out and I remembered what had been said about me being a preacher.

I still had to go back to court for the drugs case and it wasn't looking good. Leading up to the hearing I made a decision that, rather than to go back to prison and continue in the miserable life of drug addiction, I would return to Teen Challenge. I was then accompanied to the court by the deputy manager, who told the judge of my progress in rehab. During sentencing the judge said that, although he was going to allow me to return to the programme, there were conditions and that I must complete it. He also stated that, if I found myself back in front of him for similar offences, the starting point of a jail sentence would be 5 years.

On my return to rehab, I did my best to stick to the rules and the programme, but I struggled with people. I certainly hated coming under the authority of anyone or being told what to do. I was also sharing a room with someone half my age, a lad from the local church called Calvin. We didn't get on and I was finding it hard to hold it down. In prison, I would have just thrown him and his stuff out of the cell, but it wasn't prison and I was called to operate with love.

This has been a weakness for me; I hate to appear soft or vulnerable. My thoughts are that if you allow any weakness in this area – you get walked on.

I decided to leave and was told that I could find myself back in prison. I decided that at least in prison I get to call the shots. This is a misconception of many who have found themselves behind walls of sorts. You think you have the ability to control what you say or do. But that's not the case, the jailor or the one who holds the keys to your freedom does.

I was given a lift to the station and encouraged to think about what I was doing. I was warned that I would pick up a drink or use. I denied it, but the truth was that I was already sitting in the pub with a beer and smoking a fag.

I still didn't see that I had a problem with alcohol; it had been my buddy for a long time. It was like a friend putting his arm around my shoulders and saying, "Are you listening to me? The heroin and the needles have to go, but you and I are cool." I never realized that they were both close associates and with one came the other. I got drunk before getting on the train back to my miserable existence.

Stealing, scoring and dealing were the structure of my day; then getting smashed on the drink and the drugs at night. My drug use was so chaotic now that the veins in my arms had collapsed and I was injecting into my groin. If that wasn't dangerous enough, the combination of strong lager mixed with opiates is lethal. I was starting to overdose regularly and would have to be resuscitated by the paramedics. I was not put off by the fear of death and continued to be reckless with the precious gift of Life. If Heaven wasn't calling, then I felt that I wasn't needed yet.

I did become aware that something, or someone, was keeping me alive, but I was not sure of the purpose of it.

There were too many coincidences for me to ignore that something behind the scenes was definitely going on. I had escaped death more times than once. I had been shown mercy over justice in and out of the courtroom. In fact, all my prayers had been answered favorably, whether I had deserved it or not.

I returned to shoplifting, not wanting to get involved with anyone that I did not trust, in particular the drug fraternity. I would go into a supermarket with a couple of laundry bags and fill a shopping trolley with choice meats. I then walked to a quiet aisle and transferred all the meat from the trolley to the bags. I then left the store and would take it to one of the many people who liked to buy half price meat. Normally, I would grab around £200 worth of steaks, chops, joints – beef, lamb and pork. I didn't feel guilty about this, as I thought that I was just taking from those who had plenty and giving to those who had least. I filled many people's freezers.

It's amazing how people will frown upon you for the dark deeds that you do, until it is beneficial to them.

Nessa's old man, Bob, was like that; he hated me and made it known publicly. But, if I had a bit of meat, some gold or fags, then he wasn't as easily offended and would take it from me. However, in fairness to him, he did help me out on other occasions. He paid an outstanding fine when I was arrested on a warrant. He gave me a job on one or two of the sites he was on. He also provided the means for me to not do extra time for an outstanding amount owed to the courts. I felt that he thought he was better than me because of his position as a sub-contractor and the money that he had. I decided to show him what I was made of too, but I took the wrong direction.

I returned to being involved with the supply of drugs and, using contacts that I made in prison, I started to accumulate wealth and possessions and worked my way up the criminal ladder to a higher position. My attitude was: 'If I'm bad, then I want to be the best at it.' I thought that I was unstoppable and I was driven by the thought of being 'stronger and determined to be the one who was better off'.

My old friend, Chris, had resurfaced after a long period away and appeared to be a more spiritual person. He told me how the Lord had given him a word about me, but he wasn't prepared to share it with me.

Sometime after, I was attending a day group called Spotlight. It was in a church hall on the outskirts of town. I still wanted to get off heroin, but I was not prepared to give up the way of life that I was living. During one of the closed groups (men only), I was sitting on a chair listening to a speaker in our group, when I saw the word 'Nebuchadnezzar' on a wall. I didn't know what it meant and asked someone in the church if they could tell me. I was told of a Babylonian king in the Old Testament. His story can be found in the book of Daniel. After rebelling against God, the Israelites were taken captive by Nebuchadnezzar. He reveled in his own power and might and was brought to his knees. He was then made to crawl through the wilderness, resembling an animal, until he acknowledged God and was redeemed.

This had quite an impact on me because I was able to see the parallels in our stories. I'm not saying and nor do I consider myself to be a king, but the implications were there; I just didn't heed the warning. Nevertheless, it was something that remained with me and I still wanted to be able to do it a different way.

God is merciful, as I have already suggested, and He does give us warnings, before He pronounces judgement. But whether it was because I learnt this from a person whom I had reason to mistrust or down to my stubbornness and rebellion, I proceeded to cause anarchy.

The point is, the law is the law and if you continue to break it, there will be harsh consequences. Just because you haven't been lifted, doesn't mean that a case isn't being built against you. The police have the biggest gang in the world and one that sticks together, whether in goodness or not. The other thing is most of the cases brought to court are either through one's own admission (at some stage or another) and/or an informant. Police rely on these for a majority of their cases and have done so for most of mine. The criminal world is not known for honesty, loyalty or integrity. In fact there is no 'honour amongst thieves'. Someone is going to sell you out and, more often than not, it's your closest companion. If you keep the company of the devil or do his work, then you are going to be left feeling robbed or disappointed. Besides that, his work is never done and he is a hard taskmaster.

Another point that I feel it's only right to mention, is that success of any sort brings contempt, in us and from others too. I was not respecting the power of the drug that had taken over so many of the lives in my community. I also didn't realize that there were those that thought I was just capitalizing with no thought to their, or my own, downfall.

There was a guy in my town that had tried to prevent other dealers from serving me and had made slanderous remarks about my character. He was dealing himself and he saw me as a threat to his business. He had approached me once to work with him as partners, but I didn't trust him and refused. This same guy then informed on me and I was approached by old bill, whilst walking through a neighbouring estate. I was carrying a parcel of drugs that I needed to get rid of and so I took off, with the police giving chase. I managed to throw the package away before being arrested. They took me to the station and gave me a full body search. This required me to take off all my clothes, while they inspected my front and rear; even getting me to bend over while one of the officers looked up my ass. They found nothing and I was released shortly after. I made the mistake of thinking that it had all gone unnoticed and I returned to the scene to retrieve the drugs. My second mistake was that I should have got another person to pick the parcel up. An unmarked squad car was parked nearby and I was soon apprehended again. I would normally go 'no comment', but was warned by my brief that this could cause adverse inference if it went to court. I decided to make a prepared statement in my defense, before giving the usual 'no comment' reply.

I did not state what the powder in the packaging was and so it had to be sent off to the laboratory to be tested. I was given bail, to return at a later date.

If I had been operating out of a sound mind, I would have heeded all warnings, but my drug induced mind was deceived and I continued to spiral out of control.

The dealing continued, but I did try other shots at detox and rehab. Towards the end of June 2006, I entered Baytrees, which is a detoxification unit in St James, Portsmouth. This is a hospital for those with mental health problems at different stages, with secure units for those who are unstable. I had been there several times before and hoped that this time would be successful. The thing is, if you keep doing something the same way, then you are going to get the same results.

Once again I had a rehab lined up, so that I could avoid another prison sentence. I treated it as a formality, meaning I established and followed a set of procedures. The truth was, although I might have kept up the appearance of doing the programme, my heart wasn't in it. I hated the thought of being stuck in a place with lots of broken people. In my mind, I was the only well person there.

During breaks between groups, the residents were permitted to go out of the grounds to the shops, providing that they were accompanied by at least one other. This is so that they can be accountable to each other. I noticed this young guy that seemed to have his head on his shoulders and asked him if he wanted to go out for a bit of fresh air. Once we were outside, I mentioned that I would love a beer. I might have been testing his response, but instead of finding any opposition I found a 'drinking buddy' and we legged it to the pub. We eventually found one that was open and assured each other that it would just be a quickie.

Almost two hours later, we returned to the detox and were stopped at the main doors. Our lateness hadn't gone unnoticed, or the fact that we were both drunk. We were asked to leave, in a taxi that had been booked for us. My first intention was to go back to Gosport, but with a detour through the city. The cab dropped us off at one of the pubs in The Guildhall and we both went inside for a beer and something to eat. We made arrangements to meet up later, after I had scored some drugs. I returned to Gosport to pick up and then made my way back to Portsmouth. I found the address that I'd been given, a bedsit in Southsea, not far from the hospital. I rang a bell and was invited inside by the guy's girlfriend. We took some drugs and later that evening I booked in at a guesthouse near the sea front. The following morning, I ate breakfast and caught a cab to Portsmouth harbour. I met the guy and sorted him out, before jumping on to the ferry across the harbour. As I walked up the ramp, I didn't see the police waiting for me. It was 8 o'clock in the morning, I was among commuters and I hadn't told anyone that I was coming over. I was stopped, arrested and taken to the cells to be searched.

Thinking back, that morning and the events leading up to it were surreal. Everything seemed to turn out the way that it had been planned, but not by my choice.

The drugs on me were found and trying to claim it was for my own personal use would not be easy. I had just less than 7 grams, in individual bags, and my prints were all over them. The interviewing officer's job was made easy, as I was already on bail for a similar amount. I was remanded on bail to Winchester and resigned myself to the fact that this was it now; my luck had run out and I was going to pay the penalty.

Back in prison, I got my head down and was given a cleaner's job on 'A' wing. My brief said that I was looking at 6-8 years and so I had to make a plan about what I was going to do, to make good use of the time. I also decided to go cold turkey, I didn't want to use or have a prison prescription for any opiate substitute. I kept myself to myself and steered clear of any trouble. This didn't go unnoticed by the screws and they seemed relieved that I had stopped fighting the system, although I wasn't doing it for them; I'd had enough!

I was able to help other inmates by taking up different positions. I was on the Race Equality team. I became a BETA rep, which helped those who needed support with benefits, employment, training and accommodation. I also trained as a listener. The Samaritans selected inmates in basic counseling skills, so that the prisoners have someone to talk to when feeling depressed or suicidal. This was a challenge for me because I loved to talk and hadn't been much of a listener.

I attended the chapel services and enjoyed Bible study on a Friday morning. I met an older couple called Peter and Joyce, who took the group. There was something fatherly about Peter and I felt at peace with him.

CHAPTER FOURTEEN

Baptised In Blood

Peter became a positive influence in my life and even helped to convince me to offer a guilty plea in court; I just had to wait to be sentenced.

I had got clean from drugs and was staying away from past associates in jail so as to remain abstinent. I had time to think about what I wanted in life and I didn't want any more of the past.

I received a letter from Vanessa stating that she'd done all my money, got rid of the dog that I'd taken off of a friend who couldn't look after it and that we were over. As much as 'Dear Johns' can be painful, I knew deep down that it was over before I received the

115

letter.

Leading up to coming away, I had assaulted Vanessa after a drunken and drug-induced binge. I had been charged and even had her turn up in court as a prosecution witness. The worst part of that for me was seeing my youngest daughter give evidence. Although I know and accept it to be wrong to hit a woman, there were some aggravating factors at the time; and Nessa approached me soon after for us to make amends. My concern at the time was that Kate looked extremely uncomfortable and upset, having to give evidence.

I hadn't been committed or faithful in our relationship and had spent too along apart from my kids. I was concerned about the threat of not seeing them again, but my girls made it known of their love for their dad. I had been blessed with an unconditional love from my children and I wanted to warrant it and have it completely deserved. I remembered the promise that I made about doing anything to make it right and this led me to make a life- changing decision.

Alone in my cell, I got down on my knees and started to pray:

"Lord of heaven and the earth, I admit that I have failed to do the things that I've wanted to do. I have made mistakes and got it completely wrong, again and again. I confess that I have sinned in so many ways and I am asking for your forgiveness. I am sorry for all that I have done and for the man that I've become. Please forgive me and, if you are really there and if you really care about me, then please help me right now, because I have had enough. You are my Lord and Saviour and I need you to help me to turn my life around. Amen."

I got off my knees and got into my bed. I had the most peaceful sleep ever and woke with a reassurance that things were alright.

Soon after, I was promoted to the position of Number One Orderly, which gave me extra privileges and undeserved favour. In all my years in prison, this position had not been available to me. I had been a bane within the system and disputed all authority.

My court hearing for sentencing was in January 2007 and I was taken to court in the sweatbox. I was uncommonly relaxed and waited patiently in the cells for my turn upstairs in front of the judge. The cell door opened and the guards were friendly as they took me upstairs to the courtroom. As I was escorted to my place in the dock, I looked up at the judge, who smiled at me. That's never an indicator of what some might presume to be favorable; I'd experienced the same when I'd received other periods of custody. Both prosecution and defense said their bit and then the judge adjourned. He returned ten minutes or so later and took his seat at the bench. I was asked to stand and His Honour began to recall all that had been said about me, both good and bad. He gave me credit for my early plea and acknowledged that, although there had been aggravating factors, I was clearly remorseful. He then went on to give me credit for the effort that I had appeared to put in whilst on remand. I was then sentenced to 3 years 6 months' imprisonment, which meant that I would have to serve half the sentence in prison. I had already done five months and that left sixteen months to do. I was pleased with the outcome and felt that I had been given a result – God is good!

I returned to jail a happy man, considering the circumstances. I could now see light at the end of the tunnel and would be out the following year before Christmas.

I asked for a ship-out to another nick, so that I could use my time constructively and positively. I wanted to do at least one vocational course and get something out of this time away from my family and friends.

It dawned on me that I had been given another chance and I was grateful to Peter for his encouragement and support. I spent a lot of time reading the Bible; in fact it had become a way of life for me. I started each day by reading a devotional called 'Word 4 Today' and the scriptures that accompanied it. I found that, through the act of this daily discipline, I was ready and prepared to face the day, no matter what was thrown at me. I had heard of Jesus before coming away, but now I was beginning to get to know Him and it was definitely good to have him around.

One morning during cleaning duties, I was mopping the floor of A Wing, as C wing prisoners were being escorted to the gym. I was approached by a lump of a lad, who was in for attempting to rob my dealer. The dealer hadn't been in and so he and three associates had terrorized an addict who was staying there. He gave a story to the other lags when he arrived at the jail but had over elaborated on the sequence of events. I had given a truthful account and he had taken umbrage and sought me out to save face.

He came up to me in front of everyone and started to shoot away at the mouth. Now in prison it's one thing not to back down, but normally it's out of sight and away from the warders. I felt on the spot and for a moment was concerned with how I might look if I didn't react according to inmate rules. I walked off to my cell and felt conflict within my soul. If I didn't sort it out, I would look like a mug or even worse – a coward. I dropped to my knees there and then. I prayed something like:

"Oh Jesus, I am in a tight spot and if you don't help me, this is going to get messy."

I wasn't prepared for His answer and I was pleasantly surprised when the lad passed by my cell door the next day and knocked. That was the first surprise. In this kind of situation, there is no knock; normally, they rush in and hit you from behind, before you can defend yourself. The guy then apologized to me and offered me his hand. I felt relieved and put out my hand in return. All the years of having to stand up for myself and never backing down, had been removed in that instant. I started to learn that I could trust Jesus and that He had my back.

Things went relatively smoothly from then on and I was soon transferred to HMP Channings Wood down in Devon.

After a few weeks there, I was placed in a workshop, which is compulsory work for new arrivals. I did, however, find favour during the induction process. They were looking for one man who could operate the computer embroiderer. I'd taken up a computer class in earlier years and often wondered what had been the purpose of it, because up till then this skill hadn't been needed. Everyone else had to be allocated to sewing machines that provided jeans for the inmates in prison. I didn't fancy the idea of being stuck at one of these machines in the first place and I didn't even have to create a fuss. My job was in a small office type room, designing the prints for embroidered T Shirts.

I spent a few weeks at that and then applied for a place on an NVQ Business Studies – Firm Start. I got accepted, contrary to a principal's objection to me serving insufficient time in the workshop. It was a Level 3 course and I did an 'English Speaking Skills' course alongside it, at the same level. I showed signs of being an entrepreneur and presented some fresh ideas for the products or service that I had in mind. Although they were accepted as viable, I was encouraged to bring something that I already had experience with. I decided to go with event management.

Years previously, I managed a group of four young guys who called themselves 'Them and Us'. They were runners-up in the 'Battle of the Bands' in the summer festival.

I was a friend and neighbour of Terry, the bass player. He had asked for my assistance and I had obliged for a short season. I gave that up as a bad experience because musicians can be very temperamental and prone to doing their own thing. Not only does this affect the harmony of the group, but it also plays havoc for the manager, especially when he books them in at a venue and they don't turn up.

I'd also been lead vocal in another group called: 'Criminal Element'. This happened purely by chance and was the result of my taking a music class in HMP Winchester. The original vocalist didn't want to sing 'Angels' by Robbie Williams and so I stood in and had to rehearse about fifteen songs almost overnight, for a gig that took place in the chapel. I absolutely loved it, although it was very daunting up the front playing to an audience of inmates and a couple of outside visitors. I did get the feel for it though and another gig was put on soon after. I also recorded and help produce a sample disc, with a couple of tracks of old cover songs on it. My youngest daughter, Kate, loved it and played it to her friends proudly.

During my time as the band's manager, I had hoped to put on a show at a local Fort and had asked English Heritage for permission. After some negotiating, my application was accepted but, shortly after, I had a serious car crash that resulted in my friend Colin's death. I had taken six months to apply for an entertainments' license because I'd also approached army camps with a view to booking a gig for the band. But my mate's death stopped me dreaming and I shut my entertainments business down.

Now, back in the classroom, looking for an idea for my business plan, I proposed 'Amadeus Enterprises'. This was accepted as both viable and, according to a projected forecast, it could be profitable too.

The idea of the course was to come up with an idea and then to completely dissect it. A business plan enables the business man or woman to see what it is they have got, what it can and will do and also what it is up against. I loved the education and after completing the course, I looked for another.

I spent a lot of my time down the gym keeping myself physically and mentally fit, but I didn't let my gym sessions interrupt my worship. I chose to miss circuit training on a Sunday because it coincided with the Sunday service. We are required to take a rest on the Sabbath and besides that I enjoyed the fellowship of coming together like brothers, laying everything down and all focused in one direction – Jesus Christ.

I found a way to get as much gym time as I liked and not miss Sunday's morning and evening services. I put myself down for the full-time gym course and got to do both (God always provides a way).

I completed the courses at Channings Wood and requested a transfer to HMP Earlestoke. I was interested in doing the 12-Step programme because I had identified some compulsive behaviour that still needed to be dealt with.

In the autumn of 2007, I arrived back at the first institution that I had started at. I had done a complete circle and a lot had changed, especially the wing that I had spent my first period of detention in.

The quality of youthful exuberance had diminished. The harsh regime that operated out of strict discipline had been replaced by an oppressive state of desecration and degeneration.

The first night on the wing, as I lay on my bed adjusting to the surroundings, a dark shadow fell across my cell door. Through the crack I heard the tempter say, "I'll give you seven for £50 and two up front. All you have to do is send it to this address and I'll give you the rest."

Now I should have told him to f--- --f. I know that doesn't sound very Christian, but you can't pat the devil. But I felt pleased with myself and thought a couple of smokes wouldn't hurt. I had the cash sent to the account given, not once, but on several occasions. It wasn't long before I started to feel the physical withdrawals and regretted what I'd done. Desperate to get back on track, I went to the office and asked for an immediate transfer to the supposedly drug- free wing.

A week later, I was on the 12-Step programme and started to take a serious look at my addiction. The sad thing is that you can't get away from drugs; they are around you and prison is no different. I saw men trying hard during the day to combat their addictions, only to fall foul at the dealer's hands at night. Every morning, in the first of the day's groups, we would 'share' how many days that we had been drug free. (Alcohol doesn't count in prison because by rights there shouldn't be any because it is illegal.)

I would be sitting across from someone stating that they were forty days clean and sober and yet I'd witnessed them smoking off the foil the previous night. But, you try not to judge because you know the very next day that could be you. I tried hard to stick with the programme, being honest, willing and open; I even obeyed the rules, such as the prohibition of drink, drugs and any other contraband. I played no part in any dealing, 'baroning' (the loaning of tobacco with extortionate interest rates) or even the use of mobile phones. I had become an almost model prisoner, but at a price. Other inmates get suspicious of your motives and you witness and experience their mistrust. This shouldn't have mattered to me but, through it, I recognized that I had been seeking approval. Rather than keeping my integrity, I followed suit and smoked some gear. The next morning I felt convicted and owned my lapse, which resulted in the program terminating for me. I was told by the care team that I should take a rest and maybe get a job in the gardens. I didn't understand it at the time but I didn't question it and applied for a job on the Farms & Gardens. I managed to get another NVQ in Horticulture and finished my time, digging and planting crops.

I was eventually moved to the top wings that are more settled and the inmates are able to wear their own clothes and have more liberty. The spurs on the units are locked from each other, but prisoners are able to move to and fro from each other.

I was given a D Cat status, but was not able to benefit from more open conditions until the time of my release, which was quickly approaching.

I had nowhere to go and was asked if I needed assistance with housing. I hoped that I might be given a flat or even put up in a nice bed and breakfast. But instead I was discharged to a hostel in Southampton, and at first I was not feeling it, being a Pompey fan.

I didn't know what I was going to do with my life; I had a list of convictions and had spent almost all my life in prison and caught up in addiction and other compulsive behaviours. I clearly heard God's voice and became aware that I was to try and prevent others from going down the same path and to help those who were already on it. I saw myself as a soldier who was behind enemy lines and on a mission to lift up those who had fallen on the battlefield.

'The Lord of heaven and earth had looked down from his sanctuary in heaven and had heard the groan of the prisoner and released him that was condemned to die: For He listens to the prayers of the destitute and He will not reject their pleas.'(Psalm 102:17-22 NLT)

God had a plan for me and He had already placed people on my path, to help me on the journey.

Peter and his wife Joyce (from the prison) were still in regular contact with me, and would come down once a month and take me for lunch.

Most of the people from the church that I became friends with were leaders. I found it ironic, how an ex-addict/offender could be accepted so openly and warmly; but that is the grace of God.

I would love to say at this stage, that I'd cracked it, but I still wasn't fully aware of whom I am in Christ. There were still issues that had to be dealt with and the removal of any addiction is just the first part; after all any addiction is just the effect of what's really going on inside us.

As a result of being a needle-user, I had played 'Russian Roulette' many times with the 'gun': It was just a question of time before the chamber became loaded and I became infected with a blood-borne virus. I had shared my injecting equipment many times in the urgency to get the drug into my blood stream.

Hepatitis C lurks around; chronic hepatitis can quietly attack the liver for years without causing any symptoms. Unless the infection is diagnosed, monitored, and treated, many of these people will eventually have serious liver damage.

CHAPTER FIFTEEN

Freedom Awaits Me

At this stage of my story, it might be worth a word of warning; the truth lies ahead and it's the truth that set me free. If you are happy to stay in the dark, then you might find the next two chapters uncomfortable.

The transition from devil's lackey to 'God's Army' is not only invigorating, but something that I am eternally grateful for. People have mocked and scoffed with the usual comments like: 'God Squad' and 'Bible Basher', but I would rather be a Christian and follow Jesus, than conform to the world and a New World Order; which by the way isn't new, it's been going on for centuries. (That's for another book though.)

Regardless of what had become of me, I was aware that there was a purpose to my survival and all that I had been taken through. I believe the words of the prophet Isaiah sums it up in:

"The Spirit of the Sovereign LORD is on me, because the LORD has anointed me to preach good news to the poor. He has sent me to bind up the broken-hearted, to proclaim freedom for the captives and release from darkness for the prisoners,

to proclaim the year of the LORD's favour and the day of vengeance of our God, to comfort all who mourn, and to provide for those who grieve in Zion - to bestow on them a crown of beauty instead of ashes, the oil of gladness instead of mourning, and a garment of praise instead of a spirit of despair. They will be called oaks of righteousness, a planting of the LORD for the display of his splendor." (Isaiah 61:1-3 NIV)

Shortly after arriving in Southampton, I moved into a shared house in Portswood. I found a church to attend that was local and started to make new friends. I spent time volunteering in the local churches and became aware of a new initiative that was soon to take place. Street Pastors is a group of volunteers from within the surrounding churches of the community. They patrol the streets on a Friday and Saturday evening, offering pastoral care to those that might find themselves in a vulnerable situation as a result of over-indulgence in drink and other substances. Their primary purpose is to assist those that may find themselves 'worse for wear' and require a safe passage home.

I enlisted and started the training that is required to fulfill this position. I met a guy called Paul O Neill, who volunteered to give me a lift each week on the training course. Despite being from different backgrounds, we hit it off and became great friends.

Earlier in my story I stated that I didn't see alcohol as the problem and that I had become very acquainted with it. It had just seemed like a way of life, although I was aware that most, if not all, of my convictions were accrued through drink or drug use. I still felt convinced that I could manage it. The trouble was it had come to be in control of me. I was still showing signs of offending behaviour and, although the court cases were becoming few and far between, I still found myself in a precarious position. It seemed that no matter how hard I tried to put it all behind me, I was constantly falling short of staying upright.

I engaged with the alcohol services and attended 12-step meetings. I was placed on drink and drug treatment orders, but failed to comply fully with all the conditions of the orders.

It didn't help that I still found myself drawn to dysfunctional relationships, something that I was familiar with. It's not just the drink/drugs that can tear us apart, but the people that we mix with – all associations must be severed. I had left the environment back home and the associates that I had 'used' with. I thought that I had left the problem behind, but I had taken it with me.

My friends at the church supported me and never once gave up trying to encourage me to press on towards the goal. Paul became a very close friend and drove me to rehab on one occasion; he never stopped believing in me. He'd collected my belongings from a detox in Elephant & Castle, London, on another occasion and then drove back up from Southampton a week later to visit me in Brixton Prison. I really wanted to do it for everyone else, including my children, but I failed to want to do it for myself. As soon as it got tough – I was off again!

I have spent much of my time in jails, but as much as being confined behind any walls is like a prison, there is nothing like living in a hostel like 'Patrick House'. These places are like the devil's playground and are not particularly good for your morale or mental health. Take a mixture of broken people and place them in a boiling pot and you have a recipe for disaster just waiting to happen.

It can be lonely and at times you can feel hopeless, as you do your best to put your life back together. Years of abuse can take its toll on the individual and their friends and loved ones. More often than not, family relationships are shattered and can be almost impossible to reconcile. It is quite common to take refuge in a place where there might appear to be no sign of rejection, but instead a welcome, esteem and some joy.

During my stay at another Southampton hostel, I met an ex-working girl, who was also a prolific drug user. At first I avoided her because I had been warned that she could be trouble and that she had preyed on many a man. We lived in the same building, but I ignored her for months, as I tried to engage in one of the drug treatment programmes. I had managed to remain abstinent for a short while, following an accidental overdose. I'd had a particularly hard day and was hoping to score some heroin. I returned to the hostel and bumped into her on my landing; she was visiting one of my neighbours. I asked her if she could get me some heroin and she refused. When I asked her why, I thought that it was because she didn't trust me. Yet, it seemed that I was not only wrong about that, but her too. She told me how well I had been doing and that she didn't want to jeopardize that. She also told me a whole lot of other things, which made me, feel that I had been harsh towards her and that she deserved a chance. I was drawn to her vulnerability and felt that I could save her from her own destruction. But instead I found myself spiraling to new depths of depravity. It wasn't the first time that I had been introduced to crack cocaine, but this girl made it even more alluring. I was not prepared for the risqué behaviour on her part, which would accompany it. This girl had come from a Muslim background, where women are considered inferior to men. She had also been labeled a slut, for letting a boy kiss her when she was very young. Her father had not given her the love or respect that was needed and men had used and abused her along the way; all she doing was, giving back what she believed and had already received. She wasn't prepared to accept that a relationship could be had without drink and drugs, nor was she willing to try one. I got stabbed twice during that relationship, which almost cost me my life and a year of pain, shame, humiliation and downright degradation. I found myself sliding down to the pit, faster than a man on a bobsled. I eventually took the advice of the church, which was backed up by scripture: *'Do not be unequally yoked.'* To be honest with you, it didn't help matters that we didn't share a dream and she wasn't interested in the good things that I was doing to turn my life around; so I broke it off between us and said goodbye to her.

I returned to rehab in order to overcome my battle with substances, but failed to see and accept my attitude towards them. If I could have continued using and not had to face or accept the consequences, then I possibly would have. I'd grown accustomed to a way of life:

'There is a path before each person that seems right, but it ends in death.' (Proverbs 14:12 NLT)

When I looked in the mirror, the same face always stared back at me and I was constantly reminded of who I thought I was. But, these new friends encouraged me to see and be the man that I could be.

Another guy that made a huge impact on my life and also helped me to accept that there was a place in church for me is Pastor Frank Brookes. He had come from a lowly background but, after turning his back on his old way of life and giving his life to Jesus, he became a missionary and spent years oversees. He was a pioneer of the 'Father's Heart' and brought the message of the gospel of Jesus Christ. When I talk about the Father's heart, I mean that the Bible tells us of how a loving God saw how His people were suffering and heard their cry from Heaven. He sent a deliverer to set His people free from captivity, time and time again. But they were a rebellious bunch and needed a saviour continually. So, God showed His love for us:

"This is how much God loved the world: He gave his Son, his one and only Son. And this is why: so that no one need be destroyed; by believing in him, anyone can have a whole and lasting life. God didn't go to all the trouble of sending his Son merely to point an accusing finger, telling the world how bad it was. He came to help, to put the world right again. Anyone who trusts in him is acquitted; anyone who refuses to trust him has long since been under the death sentence without knowing it; And why? This is because of that person's failure to believe in the one-of-a-kind Son of God when introduced to him. (John 3:16 the Message Bible)

Up to meeting Frank, I didn't really think there was a place in church for a person like me; I was a serious offender. I used to think that being a Christian was just a crutch for the weak, the sick and the lonely. I also had the disposition that it wasn't for the bad guys but the good and I wasn't one of them. Frank helped changed this view of mine and he did it all with love.

A monthly 'Transformed' meeting was coming up and I had invited a drinker called Carol and her boyfriend to come with me. On the evening in question, I turned up at the hostel to take them to the meeting. Whilst there, a guy who also lived in the house approached us and made a derogatory remark to the boyfriend. He asked him, "How much would it be to have a go on Carol?"

I was appalled at this dude's behaviour and had heard a lot of complaints previously about him trying it on with a younger female resident and bullying all the other residents. I had to walk away because I could feel myself starting to bite. I walked into the reception and standing at the counter was an old drunk talking to a member of staff. The next minute the guy causing all the offence walked in and placed a burning cigarette butt on the collar of the old drunk, without him even noticing. Before the old drunk could feel it or be burned, I flicked it off and said to the assailant, "You ought to learn some manners." He replied mockingly, "Not from you, Christian boy." I totally lost it and offered him outside. He walked out behind me and squared up to me with his large frame. I instantly threw a left hook and it connected on his jaw with a devastating thud; he hit the floor. But, whatever was in him, drug-wise or some other intoxicating spirit, compelled him to get up and give it some again. So, I hit him a second time and this time launched him off his feet into the air. It was as if he was floating mid-air before landing back down on the floor. Twice he was knocked out, but he got up a third time and I felt that I was going to have to seriously hurt him and that was something I didn't want to do. The hostel staffs were concerned and called an ambulance, which arrived just before I left. I went on to the meeting alone and asked Frank if he could arrange a lift to pick up the couple. I also told him what had happened and the reason why I could not go back to the hostel, which was in case I got arrested. Frank had a big heart and looked for the good in a person. He arranged for them to be picked up and ushered me into the church. The thing is that couple nearly never made it to that night's meeting, which would have meant that Carol would not have made a decision to ask Jesus into her life that night.

Frank started up 'Transformed', which is a group of ex-offenders that have turned their back on their crimes and are now walking in faith in the work that was done at the cross of Calvary. They have asked Jesus into their lives in accordance with forgiveness of their sins and asked Him to lead them in paths of righteousness. Their testimonies are a witness to what God has and will do if you ask Him to come into your life and enable you to be the man or woman that you're meant to be.

At this stage, I understood and acknowledged the message of the gospel, but I still found it hard to let it be manifested in my own life.

I decided that I had to stop going back over old ground and to press on towards the goal. First the physical dependency had to go and then I could work on whatever I was trying to hide or run from.

It was arranged and set up for me to do a home detoxification, but first I had to find someone who would spend time with me during the initial alcohol withdrawals; which can result in heavy fitting, even death.

Fortunately, I had been getting to know the Street Pastor coordinator, Richard; He facilitated a men's lunch during the week. He volunteered to be my companion during the first 48 hours and we spent the evenings talking and finding familiar ground. He became another good friend and I was starting to have some rigid support in my life.

My pastor at Portswood Church in Southampton had recognized that I had a lot of friendships within City Life Church and suggested that I might feel that I would like to attend there. I appreciated his blessing, as I was not looking to hop from church to church. I do believe that the Lord provided shelter in different parts of the city and helped me to form important relationships that would fulfill the calling on my life.

It was at City Life, that I met a lovely young couple called Adam and Hannah. These beautiful people took me into their home and we became the family that I had been missing; they even gave me a little brother called Seth.

Before moving in with them, I had been living in a studio flat that had been obtained for me by a guy called Jim who worked in the probation service. I had completed a detoxification from Suboxone. In sixteen years or so, I had been physically dependant on opiates or a substitute, but now I was free from it. I even managed to get my first full-time job in so many years too. I got a position as a door fundraiser and worked for charities such as the Anthony Nolan Trust and Cancer Research UK. I excelled and hit targets, which meant I was promoted quickly to a team leader.

Whilst living at Adam and Hannah's, I still started to drink during the weekends, as it became a part of my job speculation to reward successful team members. I started to spiral because just a mouthful of lager, would incite me to do more. It wasn't long before I had to take voluntary leave from my job, to enable me to remain sober. The truth is I still didn't want to give up drinking entirely.

Yet God had sill decided to use me as a witness of His amazing grace. I was walking through town one evening and I came across a young girl begging outside Tesco's. I knew her family through drunken episodes in the city park. Both her mum and dad were ex-addicts, but still had a chronic alcohol addiction. The girl's name was Jewel and I'm sure that she was precious to

Jesus because he answered a very specific prayer that I prayed for her that night. She had asked me for some money and I told her that I didn't have cash to give her, but I'd give her something more important. I prayed that she would be filled with the Holy Spirit and that her desire for drugs would be lost. I walked away and went to a Transformed meeting and continued to pray for her. The next day, for no apparent reason, I went to the Day Centre that helps house the homeless. At the reception I met Jewel, who told me that, after I had left her the previous evening, she had no longer desired to use, but had decided that she wanted to go to rehab. The staff behind the counter looked on uninterested. I took her to one side and told her that there was a Christian community in Birmingham that helped people recover from all kinds of abuse and addictions; and if she was fortunate that she might be able to go there. All she had to do was ring them up for an interview and, if she was accepted, then she just had to wait for a bed to become available. I had to attend a probation appointment and so reassured her that I would return in about an hour, if she needed assistance. Once again, I prayed for this precious child and asked God to be merciful and grant Jewel the grace that she needed. On my return to the Day Centre, I found Jewel in the best of moods and she was leaping about with joy. I asked her what she was so happy about and she said that not only had she been accepted, but the staff at the Day Centre were astounded and prepared to take her to Birmingham that very afternoon. Another prayer of mine had been answered.

As a result of my drinking, I had to move out of the young church family's home and found myself homeless again. My friend, Richard, and his wife and family had bought a farm with another Christian couple. I was allowed to stay there for a short time, while once again considering another chance at Teen Challenge. The centre is always prepared to offer hope and a home for those that are lost or broken. Another interview was arranged and I attended with Richard. I arrived once again and took up an available bed, hoping that this time I would find the answer.

I returned to Southampton a month later, seventeen months short of completing the programme. I visited the Day Centre, a place for the homeless who are seeking accommodation, and applied for a flat. I found favour in the eyes of the Lord and the Street Homeless Team and was given another studio flat in a shared house. My room was on the top floor and I even had a skylight looking up at the sky and the stars at night; for a short time I was content.

I then returned to the 12-Step Recovery Courses that are usually held every Wednesday night at the Victory Gospel Church. I had attended other 12 Step meetings, but I had felt a lack of unity when there was mention of: 'a God of your own understanding'. The Recovery Course is different because it acknowledges and accepts that Jesus is our deliverer and through Him and Him only, can salvation and redemption be found. I had attempted to engage in and complete recovery courses many times, but struggled with submission in most areas. It wasn't until I was prepared to fully submit to a God that loved me and wanted the best for me that I'd finally get to see the results of the freedom that can be found in Christ.

I witnessed huge changes in my life and in my own behaviour, which I cannot take any credit for. The times when I have walked in my own strength, I have rarely, if ever remained sober or drug free. I also started to feel less self-centered and my thoughts were turned to other people in similar circumstances.

I volunteered with the drug services and was offered a role within REWIND (Real Experiences with Individual's Negative Developments). My friend, Jim, from probation had introduced this initiative and became the coordinator. We would go to schools and colleges and share our testimonies on overcoming substance misuse and offending behaviour. We worked alongside the Youth Offending Team and helped to address the issues of the young offenders. We also accompanied young offenders on Access courses run by The Prince's Trust. These are outdoor activities that are used to help individuals to manage their emotions and gain confidence, as well as other key life skills. I loved it and felt that this was what I wanted to do.

A high point for me was being interviewed by Hampshire Police, at one of the colleges where REWIND was giving their talks. 'Operation Fortress' was a crack down on drugs within the community. As a former drug dealer and user, I was able to bring a positive message to those that are struggling through the misuse of drugs and the offending behaviour that it brings on all, including the community that we live in.

My life was starting to turn around now and I met a wonderful woman called Bev, whilst attending a conference at Victory Gospel Church. We had seen each other previously at an evening group that we had both attended, but I hadn't made a very good impression on this classy 'Scouse' girl.

On the night in question, everyone else in the group had been given a chance to speak, including me, and then it should have been Bev's chance to talk. Apparently I was rude and cut her short, which had left her with a bad impression of me.

Fortunately, I was given another chance and Bev invited me back to her daughter Amy's for a cup of tea. Her son, Alex, had just moved down from Watford and Amy had been exploited by some young thug. Bev had been concerned with how Alex was going to deal with it and had asked my advice. The aggravating factor was that Amy had been diagnosed with cerebral palsy and had been confined to a mobility wheelchair. This meant that she was restricted from getting out and meeting new friends. So the indecent scoundrel took her warm welcome into her home and exploited her friendliness as a weakness and stole her expensive mobile phone and was taking £100 a week from her. In the past I would have taken the same view as Alex and wanted to dish out some physical justice. I am, however, going through a transition and decided to ask Alex to take a different approach.

Bev and I continued to see each other and she became a rock for me, in times of trouble. It was as if the Lord had sent this beauty down, so that he could show a real tangible presence of love in my otherwise miserable existence – she even saved my life.

One evening back at my flat, Bev called and asked if I was going to the Recovery meeting at church. I planned on being a little reckless and feigned sickness. That evening I went out and bought a couple of cans of beer and it weren't long before I was craving something stronger. I got hold of a dealer's number and arranged to meet and score some heroin. As I was waiting outside his apartments, my phone rang and it was Bev asking me if I was at home. She wanted to come round and talk to me about a conversation that she'd had with the course facilitator, Noel. I didn't want her to come round and I said, "No." It didn't take her long to realize that I was not being completely honest and she hung up. I went back to my flat and injected the heroin. I don't remember much after that, until I was suddenly wide-eyed and conscious of Bev being in my room beside my bed. I had slipped into unconsciousness and Bev had arrived just in time to pray over me and rebuke any spirit of death. I'm now going to share Bev's account of events in her own words:

"After the first call with Mark, I went to the meeting and asked if they could excuse his absence, due to his sickness. (First lie of his.) I thought I'd give him another call and tell him what Noel had said about not having a relationship with him whilst on the course. He said that he was at home in bed (second lie) and that he didn't want any visitors. I eventually got the truth out of him and decided that I wouldn't put up with this kind of behaviour. During the course of the evening, I felt the Lord wanted me to ring him, but I ignored any compulsion to. I then heard the Lord distinctly say: "Ring him." I refused and told the Lord that he had lied to me and I wasn't going to put up with a liar. I eventually went to bed, but was woken up abruptly and the Lord commanded that I ring him: 'Now'. I obeyed the Father and phoned Mark. He answered the phone, but it was hard to understand him, as his speech was slurred and incoherent. I decided to visit him at his flat and check that he was okay. When I got there, he was acting very strange and I was concerned for his physical and mental state. He then lay down on his bed, closed his eyes and took a bad turn for the worse. I asked him if I should get an ambulance, but I wasn't getting any sense from him. He then seemed to slip into a coma and I didn't know what to do, as I'd not had any experience with drug users in this state before or with how to revive them. I called upon the Lord to help me and was led in a deliverance prayer. Mark came round and wasn't aware of what had just taken place. This upset me but I was glad to see that he had recovered, as I had been sure that he was dying."

I owed Bev my gratitude and my life, but I wasn't prepared for the song of praise that came out of my heart. It could only have come from the Lord!

This was not the only miracle to take place when Bev came into my life. I'd witnessed and experienced more, but the one that stands out for me is the healing from a particular nasty virus. I'd started to attend Victory Gospel Church on a regular basis with Bev and enjoyed the worship there. During a particular service, Pastor Ron (the founder of this church) was preaching about the Kingdom. He suddenly stopped what he had been teaching on and said, "There's someone here that God wants to heal from a blood disease." I didn't need any prompting to respond because I'd since found out that I had contracted Hepatitis C and I felt like a leper with it. I went to the altar and he laid hands on me and rebuked and cast out any spirit of sickness, infirmity and disease. I walked away from the altar, thanking God for the manifestation of my healing, before I'd experienced it. Sometime after this meeting I attended an appointment at the hospital to have blood tests and see a specialist in this field. The doctor said that, although I had incurred a large strain of the virus, she wasn't sure whether I should be treated for it. I asked her why and she told me that it had unnaturally gone down to a weaker strain. This was my chance to step out in faith and declare my healing. I declared and decreed that God had been merciful and would heal me of Hepatitis C. I then bade her farewell and left her office, confident that the Lord would answer my prayer. Two weeks went by and then I received a letter from the hospital that pronounced excellent news. The blood borne virus had disappeared from my blood, without leaving any trace. I was given a clean bill of health – praise the Lord.

All the years of alcohol and drug abuse had made such a huge impact in my life and the devastation that had been left behind was catastrophic. I accepted that I was going to need much healing and deliverance, if I was going to be the man that I was called to be. I believe that God had seen my pain and heard my cry from the 'pit'. His answer was to send me a companion and helper in Bev and He was going to have to equip her and strengthen her for the journey. We would spend many more days and nights before I was going to experience the freedom that my soul was deeply searching for. I asked Bev if she'd commit to me and we became engaged.

Around the same time, a young boxer called Matt, from City Life, asked me if I'd like to accompany him on a coaching course in boxing skills. It was an ABAE registered training course and would enable me to coach some of the youth from a neighbouring estate. Every Monday night we set some bags up in the church and put the lads through some rigorous training. I recognized some of them from the schools that I had visited through REWIND and it was good to follow up with some down time with them.

I even saw a friend of mine; called Jay, get healing and deliverance, which meant reconciliation with his son. Bev and I took him off the streets, gave him a home and asked God to show him the plans that He had for Jay to prosper and give him hope. As a result of this, our vision for 'Kingdom Keep' was born.

Bev and I married on the 3rd November 2014 at Southampton Registry Office. It was a simple affair with just a couple of close friends and we planned on having a church blessing later, for our family and other friends. It was an emotional time for me, as I stood at the wedding altar and watched my wife-to-be walk into the room. We had chosen an old song by Etta James called '*At Last*' and it was very appropriate to how I felt about my newfound love; for the very first time, I was actually crying with joy.

I'd found happiness and things were starting to turn around for me. I had a different kind of life ahead of me and it was time for Bev and I to start to make plans for our future together.

All I had needed was some faith, but when faith is replaced with unbelief and when God's will is set aside for self-will... the difficulties and problems of life become insurmountable and everything seems to fall apart. But when Christ is seated in His rightful position on the throne of our heart we have God's never-failing promise... that He will lead us along the right path and guide us through every problem we may have to face.

CHAPTER SIXTEEN

One Last Fight

I couldn't believe that there was a God that cared about me. I couldn't believe that He would care about me so much that He would send His only begotten Son to die for me. I mean, I am naturally sinful, selfish, rebellious and disobedient. And yet the truth has been revealed that, while I was separated from God, I was in darkness and there was no light. Yet, when I was willing to take a step of faith, I'd be brought out of darkness, oppression and captivity and restored to a position of righteousness through faith.

My thoughts started to turn back to the memory of my own father. My dad had been troubled and I don't know to what extent his past may have contributed to it. I do know that my own dependency on porn opened a portal for perverse and wicked things to enter. I do know that the threat and acts of violence that I suffered from his hands were not of God and so I can only conclude that my father was oppressed by something that is evil. I do believe that he repented, as it was evident in the way that he finally spoke to me and the way that he loved my brothers towards the end. But, it was because of the brokenness in my relationship with my dad, that I found it hard to accept at first that there was a loving Father in heaven.

You might find it hard to believe that there is a devil or a God, but I have come to know their work personally in my life. You only have to look back and see how a malevolent force was at work in the beginning. My mum and dad's marriage appeared to be a sham and was in ruins before it had even begun. Something undetected wreaked havoc within them and any attempt to find happiness together was lost before the union. There was an undermining influence that was detrimental to the fulfilling of a natural and loving relationship. My mother may have just been trying to get away from her domineering mother and possibly looking for the love that she hadn't had from her own father, who was deceased. My dad, on the other hand, had been exposed to the occult through his own mother, who was a psychic medium, and I'm not aware of the relationship that he may or may not have had with his own dad. He'd also opened a door in his soul to porn, which had allowed a portal to open and invite all that would destroy marriage, like fornication, perversity and other corrupting spirits. Not to mention the worship of the occult through the Ouija board.

Both my father and mother have inherent qualities, both good and bad, but it is man's fallible nature and ability to think that he can be made whole through anything external to his own soul. To think that if we marry the right person, then we will automatically be made whole is unreasonable, illogical and untrue. To put one's own expectations on another to complete that which we are called to do is unfair and unjust. Our souls are deep and wonderfully complex and at times can incur wounds. Who else is able to know what has been put upon us by past hurts, such as abuse and/or rejection?

There are many alternative therapies and programmes that help people to address their issues. Mostly, they suggest that new behaviours can be learnt and faulty beliefs are to be challenged; but they offer only superficial treatments for a person's mortal wounds.

Here in the present year of 2016, we are experiencing a spiritual decline on a grand scale and more than ever before. God is being removed from our society and our communities and replaced by ungodly things that can't help nor save us. The effect of this is broken hearts and lives, which are being subjected to a form of captivity and oppression. Man is at war with his neighbour, nation against nation, as well as all the natural disasters, but there is an enemy closer to home that we have to contend with.

'Families are being torn apart and the consequences of this, are one parent families that lack the moral and financial support that enable them to offer the security and stability within a home; offending, alcoholism and substance abuse have become a common practice.'

Even the media and music industry often send out the wrong message, but it is still received by those that neither have positive support or the belief that there can be any other way than that which the 'world' portrays.

Having spent years at different attempts to find what my soul was searching for and encountering nothing but pain and disappointment, I am starting to walk in freedom and away from all that had been tormenting me. I've been given a home, a loving wife and an extended family throughout the church of Christ. I am also aware of my purpose in life. I have become passionate about those that have 'fallen' and are in a place of brokenness. The effects of a broken home are catastrophic, but the effect of being separated from God is eternal. The devil (Satan) is at work to undermine and to tear at the very thread of society. He is a despicable foe that comes undeterred in an attempt to destroy all that is good, moralistic and true. His will is to desecrate all that was created to be.

At first I chose to be wayward. I was running away, trying to escape former things and to protect myself from any hurt that I might face again. But, instead I became full of guilt, shame and an intense fear of separation. I was left in a worse state than before. I found no answers in the idols (drugs, money and power) that I'd worshipped. All the money that I felt I had earned was taken from me or spent. I had no power, but instead became powerless. The only position I found myself in was a dark and desolate place.

In the Bible, in the book of Exodus, it tells the story of Hebrew slaves being in captivity and under the rule of oppressive slave masters. They cried out to God for a deliverer and found freedom through a godly man called Moses. I had allowed myself to be led into a form of slavery too; but I heard the call of God and, in the words of the 'weeping prophet' Jeremiah:

"Come home to me again,
for I am merciful.
I will not be angry with you forever.
Only acknowledge your guilt.

*Admit that you rebelled against the LORD your God
and committed adultery against him
 by worshiping idols under every green tree.
Confess that you refused to listen to my voice.
 I, the LORD, have spoken!"*

*14"Return home to me, you wayward children."
 22" My wayward children," says the LORD,
 "come back to me, and I will heal your wayward hearts."
(Jeremiah 3:12-14 & 22 NLT)*

Like the people of Israel, I saw that I could be stubborn and rebellious. It was time for me to repent and ask God to heal my aching heart. I also knew that I had been in a place of oppression and captivity; I needed deliverance as much as the Hebrews in Egypt. There had been no one else around that could help me break free from the chains of bondage; I looked for a higher power and found it in the God of Israel and His one begotten son - Jesus. He answered my prayer and is leading me in His promise of better things. I have witnessed His wonders and many blessings, but it has not been without a fight. Although the fight is not mine anymore and, like Pharaoh of Egypt, my enemy is the devil; but Jesus Christ is the deliverer:

"There is salvation in no one else! God has given no other name under heaven by which we must be saved." (Acts 4:12 NLT)

I too had spent too long in the wilderness, due to my own mindsets, but I've had to take captive every thought that says: *'I can't do this',* or *'It's never going to happen';* and *'I don't believe it!'*

Joyce Meyer wrote a good book that's well worth a read; it's called: 'Battlefield of the Mind: Winning the Battle in Your Mind'. I could list a variety of books that I've read that may be of interest, but I want to stay focused on the message that I'm trying to give here.

First of all, you have to believe in something that you want to see and then you have to have faith in it happening. If you allow fear, doubt or anxiety to take the place of what you believe in or to stop any faith in receiving it, it isn't going to happen.

Faith is a necessary requisite that determines, demonstrates or tests the strength of a person's convictions. For it is by grace that I have been saved, through faith and this is not from myself, it is the gift of God. As a result of asking God to forgive me and receiving salvation through His Son, I now warrant His unmerited favour and have faith in Him completing the works within me.

'Now faith is confidence in what we hope for and assurance about what we do not see.' (Hebrews 11:1 NIV)

There are two types of faith that I want to mention – saving faith and the spiritual gift of faith. True saving faith involves repentance from one's sin and a complete trust in the work of Christ to save one from sin and make one righteous. Faith comes as a result of the regenerating work of the Holy Spirit. He quickens our hearts to believe.

The spiritual gift of faith is what accompanies a believer who puts his trust in God and walks or works according to His will. Those with the gift of faith trust that God is sovereign and He is good. They take Him at His Word and put the full weight of their lives in His hands. They expect God to move and are not surprised when He answers prayer or performs a miracle.

I have already mentioned the effect of walking or working in accordance to my own self-will, as opposed to walking in God's will for my life. This has been because my faith has been, at times, replaced by fear, which in turn led me to doubt and even to become anxious. All of which are crippling and contributing factors that prevented me from walking 'straight' and from being bold and courageous. That's not to say that I'm not responsible for my actions; there have been times when I could be small, foolish and immature and have not handled or controlled my emotions in an adult manner. But, as the apostle Paul writes:

"I don't mean to say that I have already achieved these things or that I have already reached perfection. But I press on to possess that perfection for which Christ Jesus first possessed me. No, dear brothers and sisters, I have not achieved it, but I focus on this one thing: Forgetting the past and looking forward to what lies ahead, I press on to reach the end of the race and receive the heavenly prize for which God, through Christ Jesus, is calling us." (Philippians 3:12-14 NLT)

I can, and will, make mistakes along the way but I now realise it's not about what I have done, can do or will do that grants me this extensive favour. It's all about what Jesus took on the cross.

Some people might think this last statement sounds a bit peculiar, but I'm talking about precious blood that was spilled for me: when Jesus' body lay stretched out on the cross, as nails were hammered into His hands; that was the punishment that He took for all my sin. I sometimes feel as though I'm continually hitting those nails into His hands and feet.

Yes, even the likes of me can find salvation and redemption. The apostle Paul also writes in his first letter to Timothy 1:15:

'This is a trustworthy saying, and everyone should accept it: "Christ Jesus came into the world to save sinners"—and I am the worst of them all.'

How great is our God that, despite all my weaknesses, sin and imperfection, He would still care more than enough to take my place. I have done some terribly sad things and yet I don't travel the walk of shame any longer because He (Jesus) did it for me at Calvary.

There was a time when I appeared to be all over the place and I had nowhere to rest my head, never mind my soul. It was quite a long and painful journey at first, but the finish is looking good. Thankfully, my hope has been restored and I've found a new place that I can call home. I have been given a new heart and a new spirit within me. God had a purpose behind the devastation that was brought about.

As a witness of what has been done for me, I am now able to share my testimony with those who are experiencing a life without hope. I have been fortunate to be part of the P.O.N (Prison Outreach Network) and go into prison and share my testimony with the inmates. I have volunteered with various ministries and organizations that work with the youth and vulnerable adults. I've given talks in schools and colleges on the development of negative behaviour and I'm working towards a healing and deliverance ministry called 'Kingdom Keep' - a stronghold where our souls can always find a safe harbour. The stronghold of God is the shelter of God.

I have a friend, who is also called Mark, and he was addicted to heroin. One day, I was checking through the posts on Face book and I read a post that captured my heart. I saw that he was homeless and sleeping in a shop doorway. On top of that he had been trying to get off opiates for years, but was struggling with a 50ml methadone prescription, given to him by the local drug services. He appeared to be vulnerable and distraught in his desolate state. I shared my concerns with Bev and we prayed for Mark. A couple of days later, there had been no sight or sound of him and so I posted on Face book a request for his whereabouts. I received a phone call from another old friend, who told me that he was at his dad's but was only staying there at night, to get out of the cold. I remembered a Christian community in Birmingham called Betel UK and I thought that there might be a chance of a bed for him, if he'd accept the help. I managed to get hold of him and tell him briefly about it. I then asked him if he'd be interested in going there and he replied that he would. I talked it back through with Bev and we prayed again, this time for wisdom. I messaged him back later that evening and offered him our sofa, while we waited in anticipation of him going to Betel. I told him that the only condition for him in staying at ours was that he trusted the process and that the detoxification began from the moment he got to ours. I wanted to see if he was motivated and committed to change. He accepted, so I got him a train ticket to come to Southampton and I met him at the station. I hadn't seen him for some time and we welcomed him into our home. That afternoon I shared some prophetic words of scripture with Mark and asked him if he would like some prayer. He was desperate and had nowhere or anyone else to go to and got down on his knees and voiced his pleas to God. I was deeply touched by his honesty, sincerity and earnestness, but I was not the only one that had heard his prayer. That evening, the three of us - Mark, Bev and I, were worshiping the Lord Jesus and I was made aware that there were evil spirits present that had been oppressing Mark. I was given the names of infirmity, affliction, addiction, sickness, methadone and other oppressive spirits. So, remembering and relying on God's word alone, I rebuked, bound and loosened those spirits from Mark and he fell to the floor. It was as if something had let go of its grip on him and he just crumpled to the ground. That night he slept peacefully and for the rest of the time at ours, until he went off to Betel. He suffered no serious withdrawals; he ate and had movement in the bowels, which had been very rare for him. I tell you the truth that this was not of my own doing. This was no act of witchcraft or sorcery, but instead through the power and glory of our living God – Jesus Christ. My pastor and other intercessors had been in prayer and by His (God's) will and by His word in Mark 16:

"16 Anyone who believes and is baptized will be saved. But anyone who refuses to believe will be condemned. 17 These miraculous signs will accompany those who believe: They will cast out demons in my name, and they will speak in new languages... They will be able to place their hands on the sick, and they will be healed." (Verses 16-18 NLT)

Mark received healing and deliverance and was able to continue his journey with the Lord. As a result of this, I am not ashamed of standing in faith and proclaiming the word of God. Only the other day, I was walking out of my house with my bible which I was carrying in its new green army fatigues case. I suddenly came to the conclusion that I have held guns and knives, but this is the most powerful weapon that I have ever carried and I'm prepared to use it. (More powerful than a light sabre and definitely a life saver)

Satan comes to steal, kill and destroy. How many of us have suffered, or are suffering, because of his subtle schemes and wickedness. We witness his destruction in our families, homes, the church, our communities and our own personal lives: in broken relationships, divorce, various forms of abuse, sickness and diseases.

This is what 'Kingdom Keep' represents; it is God's stronghold and the gates of hell will not prevail. Once we have found this place, nothing we encounter in life can defeat us; God Himself preserves us in all things. In every distress or devilish plot set against us, we emerge the better for it. It is the redemptive power of Christ, reversing the plans of the devil and annulling the effects of death in our lives.

In my past, I acted in ignorance and I was deceived. I also let pain and fear dictate my decisions. Yet, now my eyes have been opened, my heart is being made more tender and responsive: and my lips are ready to proclaim the good news of the gospel according to Christ and the work that was done at the Cross. Amen.

My book is coming to a close now and I'm sure that I have provoked thought of some kind. There will be some that mock and scoff; others will be cynical about my faith in Jesus, as I was too at one time. But I've shared with you what I've learnt through experience and the results that I've seen with my own two eyes. This was when I placed my trust and believed in the God that I had heard about. I asked Him to show Himself and I was pleasantly surprised when He turned up and told me He had a plan for my life.

"For I know the plans I have for you," says the LORD. "They are plans for good and not for disaster, to give you a future and a hope." (Jeremiah 29:11 NLT)

This is a promise for you too! If you are struggling with something, or you know someone else who is struggling, it doesn't matter whether its sickness, disease or poverty in any way, shape or form – it isn't of God. Go to a church, speak to a pastor. Get some prayer from one that moves in the power and authority that is credited to the believer. And, when one or two come together and unite in their faith, a blessing will come and touch the individual's life for the better.

I am blessed because I have a mighty woman of God who became my wife. When I'm not standing in faith, she's quick to remind me. My wife, Bev, has an anointing of healing and I have received much from God - through her. I appreciate that this Godly woman sacrificed herself when she committed to me. No other woman on earth has been able to put up with me, not even my own mother. My daughters, Max and Kate, love me and you can't beat a daughter's love for their dad – it's priceless. However, they didn't really get to choose who would be their father. But, I have chosen to love mine!

"I love the LORD because he hears my voice
and my prayer for mercy.
Because he bends down to listen,
I will pray as long as I have breath!
Death wrapped its ropes around me;
the terrors of the grave overtook me.
I saw only trouble and sorrow.
Then I called on the name of the LORD:
"Please, LORD, save me!"
How kind the LORD is! How good he is!
So merciful, this God of ours!
The LORD protects those of childlike faith;
I was facing death, and he saved me.
Let my soul be at rest again,
for the LORD has been good to me.
He has saved me from death,
my eyes from tears,
my feet from stumbling.
And so I walk in the LORD's presence
as I live here on earth!

I believed in you, so I said,
"I am deeply troubled, LORD."
In my anxiety I cried out to you,
"These people are all liars!"
What can I offer the LORD
for all he has done for me?
I will lift up the cup of salvation
and praise the LORD's name for saving me.
I will keep my promises to the LORD
in the presence of all his people.

The LORD cares deeply
when his loved ones die.
O LORD, I am your servant;
yes, I am your servant, born into your household;
you have freed me from my chains.
I will offer you a sacrifice of thanksgiving
and call on the name of the LORD.
18 I will fulfil my vows to the LORD
in the presence of all his people—
19 in the house of the LORD!" AMEN

(PSALM 116 NLT)

Epilogue

I just want to finish with a show of appreciation to all those that never gave up or turned away from me; but instead encouraged and still support me to this very day. I am in debt to a whole host of lovely people and, to some, I may not get to say thank you. I appreciate the time that you spent with me on my journey and the patience that you mostly exhibited to the 'renegade' that was within. To all the lovely people who had faith and shared their love with me and have invested and sacrificed much to see this man set free – I love you all and I am grateful that you stood by me; especially to Paul and Peter, you have become more than just valuable friends to Bev and me.

I want to express my heartfelt apologies to everyone that I have hurt, harmed or offended in my life and I do hope that wasn't during reading this book. Especially my daughters Amber and Noami, who never got the chance to see the dad I could be, As for Maxine and Kate, sorry girls, you're stuck with the one you've got, but I've sure learnt to love you more. Mum, I hope that we can meet up one day soon and that we can be reconciled in love.

To all of you who have played a part in my positive development and spiritual growth (some of it was pleasant at times), a big thank you. There are so many others that I haven't named, but I am grateful for all your support.

Finally, to my wife – it is finished (the book)! It's taken a couple of years to complete this bit of work, but I hope that we enjoy the rest of our lifetime in finishing all that is left for us to do. I love you, Beverley Anthony, and I've appreciated, and I am grateful for, your wisdom and strength. It's been tough, honey. I know that you must have thought about walking away. But you made a decision back then to stick with me and it's come at a price.

I hope that this book blesses others, as I have been blessed by you, Father. Amen!

Authors Note

Has anyone ever told you that God loves you and that He has a wonderful plan for your life?

I have this thought, that if I was to die today and there was nothing at the end of my life here on earth, it wouldn't matter so much because I would be dead and my good deeds wouldn't have gone unnoticed. On the other hand, if I choose not to believe that there is a God and neither accepted the pardon that He has given me as a free gift; I could end up in a place I'd rather not be and it would be too late to do anything about it – wouldn't you agree?

If you would like to receive the gift that God has for you today, then just say this prayer after me, with all your heart and lips out loud:

'Dear Lord Jesus,

Come into my heart. Forgive me of my sin. Wash me and cleanse me. Set me free. Jesus, I thank You that you died for me. I believe that You are risen from the dead and that You're coming back for me. Fill me with your Holy Spirit. Give me a passion for the lost, a hunger for the things of God and a Holy boldness to preach the Gospel of Christ. I'm saved, I'm born again, I'm forgiven and on my way to heaven because I have Jesus in my heart, Amen.'

As a minister of the gospel of Christ; I tell you today, that if you have prayed this prayer, that all of your sins are forgiven. Always remember to run to God and not from God because He loves you and has a great plan for your life – praise the Lord!

Printed in Great Britain
by Amazon